Coster Girls & Mudlarks
is a unique collection of authentic
voices from the streets of Victorian
London. Costermongers and crossing
sweepers, watercress girls and ham
sandwich boys, bus drivers, street
photographers and acrobats – all
speak directly to us, and provide a
compelling insight into life as it was
150 years ago.

Most of the extracts in this anthology
are from journalist Henry Mayhew's
interviews with Victorian Londoners,
although it also contains material
from other sources together with
contemporary photographs and
illustrations, notes, and an index.

Coster Girls & Mudlarks

Coster Girls & Mudlarks

Street voices
from Victorian London

A selection of nineteenth-century source material
based on interviews from
London Labour & the London Poor
by Henry Mayhew

Edited by Belinda Hollyer

For Robert Cox
who gave me the idea for this anthology

Scholastic Children's Books,
Euston House, 24 Eversholt Street,
London NW1 1DB, UK

A division of Scholastic Ltd
London ~ New York ~ Toronto ~ Sydney ~ Auckland
Mexico City ~ New Delhi ~ Hong Kong

Hardback edition first published in the UK by Scholastic Ltd, 2006
Paperback edition first published in the UK by Scholastic Ltd, 2007

10 digit ISBN 0 439 96084 3 (hardback)
13 digit ISBN 978 0439 96084 7 (hardback)

10 digit ISBN 0 439 96085 1 (paperback)
13 digit ISBN 978 0439 96085 4 (paperback)

Printed and bound by Nørhaven Paperback A/S, Denmark

2 4 6 8 10 9 7 5 3 1

CONTENTS

DISCOVERING VICTORIAN LONDON

No one alive today can remember what life was like in Victorian London. Queen Victoria inherited the British throne in 1837 and died in 1901, so there might still be a few people, living now, who were born at the end of Queen Victoria's reign. But they would have been babies when she died, and too young to experience it for themselves.

How can we discover what it was like to live in those times? In some ways it's easy, because we are still surrounded by so much evidence of Victorian England. The remnants of the world the Victorians created are everywhere – from the grand town halls and churches of the rich, to the narrow cobbled streets and tiny 'back-to-back' houses of the industrial poor. There are hundreds of books, and thousands of paintings and photographs, about Victorian England. Many museums specialize in Victorian times, many modern films and novels do the same. And some of the ideas that flourished in Victorian England – especially the opinions about economic and social prosperity – still exist today.

The middle section of this nineteenth-century photograph is on the cover of this book. The children are posing with a costermonger's cart. Only one of them has shoes to wear and the London slum that surrounds them looks bleak. What do you think the boy on the left is holding in his arms?

In human terms, however, it's harder to discover the truth. It is people, and not buildings or ideas, who make history, and their beliefs and feelings have an enormous effect on what they do and say. Because of that, it can be difficult to understand people from past times. They are a lot like us, but they aren't us in fancy dress, and we are not them with an extra helping of technology. Victorians didn't all think or behave in the same way, of course – any more than modern people do – but they were deeply affected by their times. The world in which we live is different in a thousand different ways from theirs.

But sometimes, if we're lucky, a voice from the past can jump through the time barrier and demand our attention. The voices in this book belong to people who lived and worked on the streets of London – the very poorest of the poor. Most of them had nothing but the small amount of money they made each day – if they were lucky enough to make any at all. But their poverty didn't prevent them from being brave, funny and honest. They speak directly about their experiences and their hopes, and you can learn a lot from what they say.

Understanding them can be difficult at times. Reading their words might feel rather like visiting a foreign country where you don't speak the language. So here's a brief guide to help you understand the people whose voices you will hear in this anthology.

Understanding Victorian Londoners

In Victorian Britain it was thought shameful to be poor, and so poor people were blamed for their own difficulties, whatever the cause. The government did not protect people from the consequences of unemployment. Unlike the citizens of modern Britain, Victorians who could not find work, or who lost their jobs, did not receive any government help. There was no paid unemployment allowance, no help to look for another job and no scheme for retraining.

If workers lost their jobs they had nothing to fall back upon except their savings. Local shopkeepers might give them credit for a while, and neighbours and friends might help out. They could make a little money from selling their possessions to a pawnbroker. When they grew old or infirm they were in deep trouble, unless their children helped them out. Very few workers were covered by insurance or private pension schemes. Working-class life in Victorian Britain was haunted by this total absence of any form of social security. Writers of the time compare the struggles of working people to those of a shipwrecked sailor trying to keep his head above water – alone, without help, and often without hope.

Any local welfare that was provided for the poor was seen not as a right, but as a necessary evil. Parish workhouses were the last resort for the homeless poor – and they were wretched places. Inmates were stripped and searched when they entered, had their heads shaved, and were given shapeless striped clothing to wear: in other words, they were treated like criminals. Charles Dickens said this about them: 'How much is conveyed in those two short words – 'The Parish!' And with how many tales of distress and misery, of broken fortune and ruined hopes, are they associated!'

About Henry Mayhew

Henry Mayhew was born in 1812 into a wealthy London family and became a journalist, writing articles for London newspapers and magazines. (He was one of the founders of a satirical magazine called *Punch*, which was published for more than 150 years.) In the 1850s Mayhew wrote a series of articles for a newspaper called *The Morning Chronicle* about the poor people who lived and worked in the streets of London. Later, these articles were collected and published as a series of four books, called *London Labour and the London Poor*.

Henry Mayhew was the first writer in Britain to record what ordinary people said about their jobs and their lives. He interviewed hundreds of people – on the streets and in their homes – and listened carefully to what they said. Mayhew often took a newspaper stenographer with him so that their words could be recorded on the spot. (A stenographer was someone who had learned shorthand, a fast way of recording speech.) No one had done that before.

The newspaper articles, and the books that followed, caused a sensation. It was not only unusual to interview ordinary working-class people at that time; it was also thought rather shocking. What's more, Mayhew did not mince his words. His articles were hard-hitting, and they revealed just how harsh life was for people on the edge of society. His work changed the way in which middle-class Victorians thought about their world.

Most of the material in this anthology comes from Henry Mayhew's books. His interviews and descriptions give a vivid picture of daily life in the streets of London. The people he talked to lived more than 150 years ago, but they sound as real as if they were speaking directly to you. Their stories do not give a complete picture of Victorian times, of course. Mayhew interviewed only people who made their living in the streets – people such as entertainers, food and drink sellers, and bus drivers. But the lives of such people tell us a great deal, and Mayhew's interviews are a unique record of his times.

The people Mayhew talked to seldom complain about their life and work. Although they often mention worries about the future, and of making ends meet, they don't sound angry or resentful – although the conditions in which they lived and worked seem shocking to us. Every day they battled against extreme poverty and overcrowded housing (or no housing at all). Their working conditions were appalling, and their opportunities were restricted or non-existent. They were surrounded by the constant threat of disease, disablement and death. But most of the people in these interviews sound resigned to the tough facts of their lives. They were accustomed to poverty, personal tragedy and limited expectations, and they seemed to accept that existence was bound to be a struggle for them.

The men, women and children to whom Mayhew talked were almost unimaginably poor by our standards. Many of them – especially the children – led hard and dangerous lives, and their stories often make grim reading. But at the same time their lively humour and indomitable spirits spring from the page, and their joys and sorrows seem as real as our own.

Money and measurements

In Victorian Britain, the currency was based on a different system to the decimal one used today.

A **pound** was worth twenty shillings. The coin for one pound was called a **sovereign**, and there was also a ten-shilling coin called a **half-sovereign**. A **guinea** coin was worth twenty-one shillings – that is, one pound and one extra shilling. Other high-value coins included **crowns** (five shillings), **half-crowns** (two shillings and sixpence) and **florins** (two shillings).

One **shilling** – often called a 'bob' – was made up of twelve **pennies**, and there were **sixpence** and **threepence** coins as well. (The coin worth threepence was called a threepenny – pronounced 'thruppeny' – bit.) But for most people, the penny was the central coin of the currency. It was made from copper-coloured metal, so pennies and the smaller coins were all known as 'coppers'.

A penny was used in words like a 'penn'orth', which was short for 'a penny's worth' – at a street stall you might ask for 'A penn'orth of sweet stuff'. A penny was not the smallest coin available, though: **halfpence** and **quarterpence** coins were also used. Halfpence was pronounced 'hape-nee', and often written as 'ha'penny' or 'ha'pence' for short. If something cost one penny and a halfpenny, you would call that a 'a penny ha'penny'. A quarter of a penny was called a **farthing**. (Half farthings were in circulation for some of Victoria's reign, but they weren't popular because they were so small.)

Before decimalization, amounts in pence were shown by the letter 'd' – so, for example, '5d' was short for 'five pennies', or 'five pence'. Amounts of pennies that use the 'p' for pennies always refer to modern decimal currency.

Penny

Threepence

1877 farthing

1878 sixpence

Threepence actual size

Farthing actual size

Sixpence actual size

Penny actual size

How much was the money worth?

It is difficult to compare the worth of a pound in the 1850s and the worth of a pound today. All we know for sure is that you could buy a lot more with one pound in Henry Mayhew's time than you can today! Most estimates put the value of a Victorian pound somewhere between £100 and £200 in today's money. If you choose a value halfway between these figures, the chart that follows shows what Victorian money might be worth by today's standards. (Don't take it too literally – the chart is just to give you an idea.)

VICTORIAN MONEY	MODERN MONEY
one guinea	£157.50
one pound	£150
one half sovereign	£75
one crown	£37.50
half a crown	£17.75
one florin	£15
one shilling	£7.50
sixpence	£3.75
threepence	£1.80
one penny	60p
one halfpence	30p
one farthing	15p

Measurements
A system called imperial measurement was used in Britain in Victorian times. This was the standard for hundreds of years, that was replaced by metric measurements in the second half of the twentieth century. The list below will help you understand the imperial measurements that are mentioned in this book.

LENGTH

12 inches = 1 foot	304.8 cm
3 feet = 1 yard	0.9144 metres
1,760 yards = 1 mile	1.6093 km

CAPACITY

20 fluid ounces =1 pint	0.5683 litres
2 pints = 1 quart	1.1365 litres
4 quarts = 1 gallon [8 pints]	4.546 litres

MASS

16 ounces = 1 pound	0.4536 kg
14 pounds = 1 stone	6.3503 kg
one gross = 12 dozen	144
8 stones = 1 hundredweight [cwt]	50.802 kg
20 cwt = 1 ton [2,240 pounds]	1.016 metric tonnes

A note about the text

Henry Mayhew's work is the main source of the material in this anthology, but other works have also been included (the writers are named with each extract, and the sources are given on pages 202–203). The text has been edited to help young, modern readers understand it, and most of it has been cut for length and reshaped for content and consistency. In a few cases, old-fashioned terms have been replaced with their modern equivalents.

It's hard to know which would be worse: leaky old boots that don't fit properly, or no boots at all. The dirty clothes on these boys look like hand-me-downs, and are probably all they have to wear, whatever the weather.

STREET CHILDREN

You might have thought it was fun on the streets of London in Victorian times, if you were a child. Henry Mayhew said that many middle-class children in his time envied the street children they glimpsed, and longed to live such apparently carefree lives. Even now, you might imagine that you could play all day with your friends. You didn't have to go to school – because there was no compulsory education, and no real schools, anyway, for the children of the poor. You didn't even have to wear shoes or wash very much: no one was very clean by modern standards, and certainly not the street children, who probably didn't own shoes anyway.

The truth is that some street children enjoyed themselves, but most of them had a wretched time. Not going to school might sound attractive – but if you had no schooling the odds were that you'd stay poor. (If you were lucky, you might be taught a bit of reading and writing and some simple arithmetic, but that's all.) Not wearing shoes or having to wash? Well, being barefoot in the winter wasn't any fun at all. Since no one washed much you probably wouldn't notice the smell, but dirt encourages vermin and spreads disease – and there was no free medicine or doctors. And above everything else, street children were hungry – *really* hungry – most of the time. If they didn't earn (or beg, or steal) any money, they didn't eat that day.

The modern notions of childhood as a time of play, amusement and learning simply didn't exist for the Victorians. Millions of children at that time had to work in the adult world as soon as they could do so – often by the age of ten. (In the industrial towns, factory workers began work at about that age.) Children from middle-class families had a much better education – especially if they were boys – but play, and leisure, were generally frowned on. Children were seen as miniature adults, and the sooner they grew up the better.

And the children of the London streets often had desperate stories to tell – of near-starvation and neglect, of brutal or drunken parents, and of intolerably harsh experiences. Henry Mayhew had this to say about them.

"A burning recollection of bad treatment"
Henry Mayhew: Street children

There is no doubt that, to many boys, the young street ruffian is a hero. These children have often known no guidance from parent, master, or relative, but have been flung into the streets through neglect, or as outcasts from utter destitution. Many children really sell in the streets, but others take up selling in order to have the better chance to steal, or the greater facility to beg. But these children cannot be blamed for their behaviour. They have been

A cartoon from *Punch* magazine in the 1860s:
Well-dressed gentleman: 'Now, little man, tell for a penny – why don't you wash your face?'
Boy: 'Lor' bless you – we never has no water down our court!'

untaught, mistaught, maltreated, neglected, trained to do wrong, or turned into the streets to shift for themselves.

The brutal tyranny of parents is shown in the beating and cursing of their children for trifling cause or for none at all. A boy perhaps endures this for some time, and then, finding it increase, he feels its further endurance intolerable, and runs away. If he has no friends with whom he can hope to find a shelter, only the streets are open to him. He soon meets with comrades, some in circumstances like his own, and goes through a course of horse-holding, *errand-running, parcel-carrying, and suchlike. And so he becomes, if he is honestly inclined, a street seller – beginning with a stock like nuts, or some such. There will be plenty to teach him to do this at the lodging-houses, where he sleeps when he can pay for a bed.*

I met with a youth of sixteen who about two years previously had run away from Birmingham, and made his way to London, with two shillings and sixpence to his name. Although he earned something weekly, he was so pinched and beaten by a stepmother (his father was seldom at home except on Sunday) that his life was miserable. This went on for nearly a year until in desperation the boy began to resist. One Saturday evening, when beaten as usual, he struck out in return, drawing blood from his stepmother's face. The father came home and listened to his wife's statement, and would not listen to the boy's. In his turn, the father then chastized the lad mercilessly. Five minutes more – and the boy, with aching bones and a bitter spirit, left his father's house for ever. This youth could neither read nor write, and seemed to possess no quickness or intelligence. The only thing of which he wanted to talk was his stepmother's treatment of him; everything else was a blank with him, in comparison – this was his one burning recollection.

Companionship and associations lead many children to a street. Many have seen little boys playing at marbles, or gambling with halfpennies, farthings, or buttons, with other lads, and who have laid down their basket of nuts or oranges to take part in the play. The young street seller has probably more ha'pence in his possession than his non-dealing playmates. He is also in possession of what appears a large store of things for which poor boys have generally a craving and a relish. Thus the little itinerant trader is envied and imitated.

This attraction to a street career is very strong among the neglected children of the poor, when the parents are absent at their work. On a Saturday morning, some time ago, I was in a flagged court near Drury Lane, which was full of children of all ages. The parents were nearly all, I believe, then at work, or on the lookout for a job as porters in the market, and the children played in the court until their return. In one corner was a group of four or five little boys gambling and squabbling for nuts, of which one was a vendor. A sharp-looking lad was gazing enviously on, and I asked him to guide me to the room of a man whom I wished to see. He did so, and I gave him a penny. On my leaving the court I found this boy the most eager of the players, gambling with the penny I had given him.

Only last week I saw this same lad hawking a basket stocked with oranges. On my asking if his father knew what he was doing, he replied that so long as he didn't bother his father he could do what he pleased, and the more he kept out of his father's way, the better he would be liked and treated.

The children of the costermongers become street dealers. As soon as their strength enables them they are required to assist their parents in their work, or sell trifles, single-handed, at the instruction of their parents. The child simply obeys his father; and the father simply rears the child.

COSTERMONGERS were street traders. They sold produce like fish, fruit and vegetables from barrows. The small barrows were pushed by hand around the streets; donkeys or ponies pulled the large barrows.

'Tossing the pie man' was one way to try to get a pie without paying for it! The pie man tossed a coin in the air, and called out his bet of 'heads' or 'tails'. If he was right about which side of the coin would land face-up, the buyer had to pay for a pie. But if the pie man was wrong, he had to give a pie away for nothing. Who do you think has won the bet in this picture?

"It's the sweetness that sells them"
Henry Mayhew: Two orphan flower girls

The flower season starts mostly with wallflowers, and ends with lavender. Some of the street vendors continue business through the winter, when they sell violets and dried flowers. One girl I saw told me that whenever her father was unable to give her any money to buy her flowers with, she got her stock-money of a washerwoman, who lived next door to her parents: either ninepence or a shilling. This money she returned when she came home from her day's work, and the woman re-lent it to her the next morning. The flowers are bought in large bunches, or else (as in the case of dry flowers) by the ounce. The bunches having been tied up, and placed in a basket, are carried through the streets.The girls cry out as they go – 'Handsome flowers, a penny a paper!' or 'Two bunches a penny, sweet wallflowers!' or 'Four bunches a penny, blooming lavender!' or 'Handsome moss roses, a ha'penny each!' Most of the flower girls take to selling other articles after the summer. Some deal in apples and oranges, and others in combs, or stay laces, or cedar pencils.

STAY LACES 'Stays' were corsets, worn by women to make them look slim. The stays were strengthened with strips of whalebone, and they laced up from under the arms to somewhere below the waist.

Some flower girls are the children of street sellers, some are orphans, and some are the children of unemployed people who prefer any course to applying to the parish for relief. These girls walk up and down in front of houses offering their flowers to anyone looking out of the windows, or stand at any likely place. They are generally very persevering and run along barefoot after likely people, calling 'Please kind lady, do buy my flowers! Oh do, please! Poor little girl.' Of the two girls interviewed the older was fifteen and the younger eleven.

❝We live on flowers when they're to be got, but it's very little use offering any that aren't sweet-smelling; I think it's the sweetness that sells them. I sell primroses when they're in, and violets and wallflowers and stocks, and roses of different sorts, and pinks and carnations and lilies of the valley. The best sale of all is moss roses, we do best of all on them. Primroses are good, for people say 'Well, here's spring again for a certainty!' and buy them. Gentlemen are our best customers. I've heard they buy flowers to give to ladies. Sometimes ladies say, 'Only a penny, my poor girl, here's three ha'pence for the bunch,' or they give me the price of two bunches for one.

We pay one shilling for a dozen bunches, whatever flowers are in. Out of every two bunches I can make up three, at one penny a piece. We make the bunches up ourselves, and we get the rushes to tie them with for nothing. The paper to wrap them costs only a penny for a dozen, or sometimes only a halfpenny. The two of us don't make less than sixpence a day unless it's

This was copied from a mid-Victorian photograph, and shows a young flower girl waiting patiently for customers. It must be cold because she's wrapped in several layers of clothing, but she has no shoes to keep her feet warm.

very ill luck. We do better on oranges in March or April, than on flowers; oranges keep better than flowers. I wish they was in all the year. **99**

This photograph was taken in 1877, and shows a group of flower sellers in the old Covent Garden Market in central London. You can see posies of flowers stacked in their baskets, with more posies held ready to offer passing customers. The heavy clothes suggest that the weather is cold or that it's still early morning.

Lavender street cry

Won't you buy my sweet blooming lavender!
Sixteen branches one penny,
Ladies fair make no delay,
I have your lavender fresh today.

Buy it once, you'll buy it twice,
It makes your clothes smell sweet and nice.
It will scent your pocket handkerchiefs,
Sixteen branches for one penny.

As I walk through London streets
I have your lavender nice and sweet,
Sixteen branches for one penny!

"Anything for a living"
Henry Mayhew: A coster lad

66My father was a waggoner, and worked the country roads. There was two of us at home with mother, and we used to play along with the boys of our court, in Golding Lane, at buttons and marbles. The big boys used to cheat and thump us if we grumbled – that's all I recollect. Father, I've heard tell, died when I was three. I once went to school for a couple of weeks, but the cove used to fetch me a wipe over the knuckles with his stick, and as I wasn't going to stand that, I ain't no great scholar. Mother used to be up and out very early, washing in families – anything for a living. We was left at home with the key of the room and some bread and butter for dinner. Sometimes when we had no grub at all the other lads would give us some of their bread and butter, but often our stomachs used to ache with the hunger and we would cry when we were very far gone. She used to be at work from six in the morning till ten o'clock at night, which was a long time for a child's belly to hold out, and when it was dark we would go and lie down on the bed and try and sleep until she came home with the food. I was eight years old then. A man as knew mother said to her, 'Your boy's got nothing to do, let him come along with me and earn a few ha'pence,' and so I became a coster. He gave me fourpence a morning and my breakfast. I worked with him until I learned the markets, and then I and my brother got baskets of our own. The two of us could make two shillings and sixpence by selling greens of a morning, and going around to the pubs with nuts of an evening, till about ten o'clock at night. **"**

"I knows how to sweep the crossing"
Punch *magazine, 1850: A boy in court*

George Ruby, a boy aged 14, was put into the box to be sworn and the Testament [the Bible] was put in his hand. He looked quite astonished upon taking hold of the book.

Magistrate:	Well, do you know what you are about? Do you know what an oath is?
Boy:	No.
Magistrate:	Do you know what a Testament is?
Boy:	No.
Magistrate:	Can you read?
Boy:	No.
Magistrate:	Do you ever say your prayers?
Boy:	No, never.
Magistrate:	Do you know what prayers are?
Boy:	No.
Magistrate:	Do you know what God is?
Boy:	No.
Magistrate:	Do you know what the Devil is?
Boy:	I've heard of the Devil, but I don't know him.
Magistrate:	What do you know, my poor boy?
Boy:	I knows how to sweep the crossing.
Magistrate:	And that's all?
Boy:	That's all. I sweeps the crossing.

Crossing sweepers were among the poorest of those trying to make a living in the city streets. The roads were thick with all kinds of rubbish and dirt – especially horse manure from the hundreds of horses used to pull carriages, buses and carts. Crossing sweepers swept all that away, so that 'respectable' people didn't get their shoes and clothes dirty when they stepped off the pavement and crossed the road on foot. There is more about crossing sweepers on page 191.

"It does seem dreadful cruel"
Henry Mayhew: The watercress business

"I'm sixty-two," said one man who had been sixteen years at the trade. "I've been a porter myself, jobbing about in the markets, or wherever I could get a job to do. Then there's one old man goes about selling watercresses, who's been a seafaring man; he's very old, he is – older than what I am, sir. Many a one has been a good mechanic in his younger days, only he's got too old for labour. The old women have, many of them, been laundresses, only they can't now do the work, you see, and so they're glad to pick up a crust anyhow. Nelly, I know, has lost her husband, and she hasn't anything but her watercresses to keep her. She's a good, honest, hard-working creature – poor old soul!

The young people are most of them girls. There are some boys, but girls are generally put to it by the poor people. There's Mary Macdonald, she's about fourteen. Her father is a bricklayer's labourer and he sends little Mary out to get a halfpenny or two. He gets sometimes a couple of days' work in the week. He's got three children to keep out of that; so all of them that can work are obliged to do something. The other two children are so small they can't do nothing yet. Then there's Louisa, she's about twelve, and she goes about with cresses, like I do. I don't think she's got a father but she has a mother alive, and she sells cresses like her daughter.

The sellers generally go about with an arm-basket, like a greengrocer's, at their side, or a 'shallow' in front of them; and plenty of them carry a small tin tray before them, slung round their neck. It would make your heart ache if you was to go to Farringdon Market early, this cold weather, and see the poor little things there without shoes and stockings, and their feet quite blue with the cold. The small tin tray is generally carried by the young children. The cresses are generally bought in Farringdon Market.

If we was to go to Covent-garden to buy 'em, we couldn't do nothing with 'em; they are all tied up in market bunches there; but at Farringdon Market they are sold loose, out of big hampers, so they give you a large handful for a penny. The usual time to go to the market is between five and six in the morning. I was there this morning at five, and bitter cold it was, I give you my word. We poor old people feel it dreadful. Years ago I didn't mind cold, but I feel it now cruel bad, to be sure. Sometimes, when I'm turning up my things, I don't hardly know whether I've got 'em in my hands or not – can't even pick off a dead leaf. But that's nothing to the poor little things without shoes. Why, bless you, I've seen 'em stand and cry, two and three together, with the cold and my heart has ached for them over and over again.

I've said to them, I wonder why your mother sends you out, that I have; and they said they were obligated to try and get a penny for a loaf for breakfast. We buy the watercresses by what is called the hand, and one hand will make about five halfpenny bundles. After they have bought the cresses, they generally take them to the pump to wet them. This is done to make them look nice and fresh all the morning, so that the wind shouldn't make them flag. You see, they've been packed all night in the hamper, and they get very dry. Some tie them up in bundles as they walk along. **99**

A Victorian artist named Hablot Knight Browne, but known as 'Phiz', illustrated many of Charles Dickens's novels. Here, Phiz shows the dawn scene at London's Farringdon Market in watercress season. The buyers and sellers are working by candlelight, with only one gaslight to help. You can see hampers and large baskets of watercress for sale, while buyers like the young girl in the foreground are sorting watercress into small bunches for sale on the streets.

WATERCRESS had been gathered throughout much of Europe for thousands of years. But early in the nineteenth century, the English became experts in its cultivation on the edges of fast-flowing rivers and streams, especially in the chalk downs between Kent and Dorset. In Victorian times, several early-morning rail services from Hampshire were known as 'The Watercress Express' because they brought the harvest to London for sale. Peppery watercress, the hotter the better, joined a group of sharp-flavoured foods that the Victorians loved to eat – such as rhubarb, gooseberries and damson plums.

"It's no use crying"
Henry Mayhew: The watercress girl

The poor child, although the weather was severe, was dressed in a thin cotton gown, with a threadbare shawl wrapped round her shoulders. When she walked she shuffled along, for fear that the large carpet slippers that served her for shoes should slip off her feet.

❝I go about the streets with watercresses, crying, 'Four bunches a penny, watercresses!' I am just eight years old, that's all, and I've a big sister, and a brother and sister younger than me. On and off I've been very near a twelve-month in the streets. My mother learned me to needlework and to knit when I was five. I used to go to school, too, but I wasn't there long. I've forgot all about it now, it's such a long time ago.

The cresses is so bad now that I haven't been out with them for three days. It's so cold, people won't buy them; besides, in the market, they won't sell a ha'penny handful now, they've risen to a penny and twopence. In summer there's lots, and cheap as dirt. I used to go down to market along with another girl, she must be about fourteen because she does her back hair up.

When we've bought a lot we sits down on a doorstep and ties up the bunches. We never goes home to breakfast till we've sold out, but if it's very late then I buys a penn'orth of pudding which is very nice with gravy.

It's very cold before winter comes on, specially getting up of a morning. I gets up in the dark by the light of the lamp in the court. When the snow is on the ground, there's no cresses. I bear the cold – you must, so I puts my hands under my shawl, though it hurts to take hold of the cresses, especially when we take them to the pump to wash them. No, I never see any children crying – it's no use.

Sometimes I make a great deal of money. One day I took one shilling and sixpence and the cresses cost sixpence, but it isn't often I get such luck as that. I oftener make threepence or fourpence than a shilling, and then I'm at work, crying, 'Cresses! Four bunches a penny!' from six in the morning till about ten.

When I gets home after selling cresses, I stops at home. I always give Mother my money, she's so very good to me, and don't often beat me. I put the room to rights, Mother don't make me do it, I does it myself. I clean the chairs, though there's only two to clean. I take a tub and scrubbing brush and flannel and scrubs the floor – that's what I do three or four times a week.

'The Watercress Girl' was painted in 1867 by Frederick Ifold. You can see the tight bunches of watercress arranged in the basket on her arm, ready for sale.

I don't have no dinner, Mother gives me two slices of bread and butter and a cup of tea for breakfast, and then I go till tea and have the same. We have meat of a Sunday, and of course I should like to have it every day. I never has no sweet stuff. Sometimes we has a game with the girls in the court, but not often. Me and Carrie takes the little 'uns. We play, too, at 'Kiss in the Ring'. I know a good many games but I don't play at 'em because going out with cresses tires me. I've got some toys at home, I've a box of toys and a knife and fork, and two little chairs. I never had no doll but I miss little sister – she's only two years old. We don't sleep in the same room, for father and mother sleeps with little sister in the one pair and me and brother and other sister sleeps in the top room. I always goes to bed at seven, because I has to be up so early.

I am a capital hand at bargaining, but only at buying watercresses. They can't take me in. If the woman tries to give me a small handful of cresses I says, 'I ain't going to have that for a ha'penny-worth,' and I go to the next basket, and so on, all round. I know the quantities very well. For a penny I ought to have a full market hand, or as much as I could carry in my arms at one time without spilling. For threepence I has a lap full, enough to earn about a shilling, and for sixpence I gets as much as crams my basket. I can't read or write, but I know how many pennies goes to a shilling – why twelve of course, but I don't know how many ha'pence there is, though there's two to a penny. When I've bought threepence of cresses I make them up into as many little bundles as I can. They must look biggish or the people won't buy them – some puffs them out as much as they'll go.

I don't know nothing about how much I earn during the year, I only knows how many pennies goes to a shilling, and two ha'pence goes to a penny, and four farthings goes to a penny. I knows how many farthings goes to twopence – it's eight. But that's as much as I wants to know for the markets. 🙶

A cartoon from *Punch* magazine in the 1860s:
Boy: 'Hallo, missus, wot are those?'
Old woman: 'Tuppence.'
Boy: 'What a lie – they're apples!'

"Customers want apples for less than they cost us!"
Henry Mayhew: A coster girl

She was a fine-grown woman of about eighteen, who had a habit of curtseying to every question put to her. Her cotton bonnet was crushed in with carrying her basket on her head, and her voice was husky from shouting her wares.

66The girls begin very early at our work; the parents make them go out when they're almost babies. There's a little girl, I'm sure she isn't more than half past seven, that stands selling watercresses next my stall, and Mother was saying, 'Only look there, how that little one has to get her living before she almost knows what a pennyworth means.'

There's six in our family, and Father and Mother makes eight. Father used to do odd jobs with the gas pipes in the streets, and when work was slack we had very hard times of it. Mother used to manage to keep us employed out of mischief – she'd give us an old gown to make into pinafores for the children and such like. She's been very good to us, has Mother, and so is Father. She always liked to hear us read to her whilst she was washing or such like, and then we big ones had to learn the little ones. But when Father's work got slack, if she had no employment cleaning for people, she'd go and buy a bushel of apples and then turn out and get a penny that way. By sitting at the stall from nine in the morning till the shops shut up – say ten at night – I can earn about one shilling and sixpence a day. It's all according to the apples, whether they're good or not, what we makes. Ah! There's many a girl I know whose back has to suffer if she don't sell her stock well, but thank God, I never get more than a blowing up. My parents are very fair to me.

This young coster woman displays her apples on a tray that hangs from her waist. Some costers sold fruit from stalls or handcarts, while others balanced baskets of fruit on their heads and walked through the streets calling out their wares.

I don't think I could forgive an enemy if she injured me very much. I'm sure I don't know why I couldn't, unless it is that I'm poor and never learned to do it. If we cheat in the street I know we shan't go to heaven, but it's very hard upon us for if we didn't cheat we couldn't live, profits are so bad. It's the same with the shops, and I suppose the young men there won't go to heaven either, but if people won't give the money, both costers and tradesmen must cheat and that's very hard. Why, look at apples! Customers want them for less than they cost us, and so we are forced to shove in bad ones as well as good ones, and if we're to suffer for that it does seem to me dreadful cruel. **"**

"I'm often out till four in the morning"
Henry Mayhew: The ham-sandwich boy

To start in the ham-sandwich street trade requires two shillings for a basket, two shillings for a kettle to boil ham in, six pence for knife and fork, two pence for mustard pot and spoon, seven pence for coals, five shillings for ham, one shilling and three pence for bread, four pence for mustard, nine pence for a basket cloth and apron, and four pence for over-sleeves – or a capital of twelve shillings and eleven pence.

"I hardly remember my father, but I believe if he'd lived I should have been better off. My mother couldn't keep my brother and me – he's older than me – when we grew to be twelve or thirteen, and we had to shift for ourselves. I was first in place as an errand boy, then I was a stationer's boy and then a newsagent's boy. I wasn't wanted any longer but left with a good character. My brother had gone into the sandwich trade and he advised me to be a ham-sandwich man and so I started as one. At first I made ten shillings a week, but things are worse now and I make three shillings and sixpence some weeks. My rent's two shillings a week, but I haven't my own things. I am so sick of this life I'd do anything to get out of it, but I don't see a way. Perhaps I might have been more careful when I was first in it, but really, if you do make ten shillings a week you want shoes or a shirt – so what is ten shillings after all? I wish I had it now, though.

I work the theatres this side of the water. I hardly know what sort my customers are but they're those that go to theatres – shopkeepers and clerks, I think. The women of the town buy off me when it gets late, for themselves and their fancy men. In summer I'm often out till four in the morning and then must lie in bed half next day. I go out between eight and nine in the evening. People often want more in my sandwiches, though I'm starving on them as it is. I stand by the night houses when it's late – not the fashionable ones; their customers wouldn't look at me, but I've known women that carried their heads very high, glad to get a sandwich.

Six times I've been upset by drunken fellows on purpose, and lost all my stock. Once a gent kicked my basket into the dirt and he was going off – but some people made remarks about using a poor fellow that way, so he paid for all, after he had them counted.

I am so sick of this life. I do dread the winter so, I've stood up to the ankles in snow till after midnight and wishes I was snow myself, and could melt like it and have an end. Time's very heavy on my hands sometimes, and that's when you feel it. I read a bit, if I can get anything to read, for I was at St Clement's School, or I walk out to look for another job. Mine's a wretched life and so is most ham-sandwich men. I've no enjoyment of my youth and no comfort, and I live very poorly. A ha'penn'orth or a penn'orth of cheap fish is one of my treats – then there's sometimes a sort of meal off the odds and ends of the ham which isn't quite view-y enough for the public, along with the odds and ends of the loaves. I wash my aprons and sleeves and cloths myself and iron them too – a man that sometimes makes only three shillings and sixpence a week and must pay two shillings' rent out of that, must look after every farthing. I've often walked eight miles to see if I could find ham a halfpenny a pound cheaper anywhere. If it was tainted I know it would be flung back in my face.

If I was sick, there's only the parish for me. **99**

THE PARISH mentioned by the ham-sandwich boy was feared by many poor people in Victorian times. The only official help available to them in hard times was run by the local authorities – or parishes – and was called the workhouse. There is more about parish workhouses on page 10.

"Butter's half the battle"
Henry Mayhew: The muffin and crumpet boy

The young muffin man carries his delicacies in a basket wrapped in flannel to retain the heat.

"People likes them warm, sir, to satisfy them they're fresh, but it can't matter so much as they have to be toasted again. I only wish good butter was a sight cheaper and that would make the muffins go. Butter's half the battle.

I turns out with muffins and crumpets in October and continues until it gets well into the spring, according to the weather. I carries a first-rate article. If I sell three dozen muffins at a ha'penny each and twice that in crumpets it's a very fair day – all beyond that is a good day. The profit on the three dozen and the others is one shilling, but that's a great help to Mother for otherwise I should only be minding the shop at home. Perhaps I clear four shillings a week – some does far better than that and some can't hold a candle to it. If there's any unsold, a coffee shop gets them cheap and puts them off cheap again the next morning. I like wet days best because there's respectable ladies what don't keep a servant, and they buys from me to save going out. We're a great convenience to the ladies – a great convenience to them that likes a slap-up tea.**"**

"I was frightened at first"
Henry Mayhew: A little boy tumbler

❝I was twelve years old last March, and play with the acrobats. I have done so for the last three years. I stand on the hands of the 'top mounter', who holds my feet and throws me about, catching me. I was frightened at first, but never am now. My father is dead. My mother – she has five of us – put me to this business. I'm allowed one shilling a day when performing, and I get my dinner with the men. My master takes the money to keep and clothe me. I am very kindly treated.

I'd sooner be in trade than this line of life, but if I am to be a tumbler, why I must stick to it. So I practise a few tricks now and then, and try to do something new. I was never let fall in performing so to be hurt. I am the only boy, except one, who plays with the street acrobats.**❞**

TUMBLER is another word for acrobat. Many entertainers in Victorian times earned a living by performing on the streets. There is more information about street entertainers – and about other acrobats, tumblers and jugglers – on page 89 and the pages that follow.

This 1877 photograph shows a chimney sweep holding expanding brushes to push up chimneys. He will hang the cloth around the fireplace, to stop chimney soot getting into the room. The boy in the background might be his assistant, although by that date a law prevented children from being forced to climb chimneys.

Chimney sweeps and children

The Victorians, like their ancestors, used coal and wood fires to warm their houses and fuel their cooking stoves. The fires produced soot – a fine dark powder – that stuck to the inside of chimneys, and when the soot built up the chimneys worked less efficiently. So the soot had to be removed.

Most chimneys need specially designed equipment to clean them, because the spaces inside are so narrow. But in seventeenth- and eighteenth-century Britain, small people were a cheaper option than special equipment. Orphanages sold children as young as four years old to master sweeps, so that they could clean chimneys. Homeless children were also tricked or forced into this terrible trade. The children were sent into a chimney to clean the soot from the chimney walls with their hands or with scrapers. Many of the children were terrified and reluctant to climb, and so the sweeps would light small fires in the fireplace to force the children to climb further. Every day children risked getting stuck in a narrow chimney, being choked by smoke and fumes, or falling to their death.

By Mayhew's time, the British parliament had passed an act forbidding anyone under the age of twenty-one from climbing chimneys. The law wasn't very successful, however, because the fines for breaking it were very small. In 1864 another act was passed with a fine of £10, which was a very large amount for the time. The police, the courts and the public supported the new law, and soon there were no more children climbing chimneys. But the old showman, whose story follows, had been a chimney boy in his young days.

"He coaxed me with pudding"
Henry Mayhew: A chimney boy remembers

A short thick-set man with small, puckered-up eyes, and dressed in an old brown velveteen shooting-jacket, gave me an account of his life.

"My father was a soldier, and was away in foreign parts, and I and a sister lived with my mother in St Martin's workhouse. I was fifty-five last New Year's Day. My uncle, a boot maker, took my mother out of the workhouse, that she might do a little washing, and pick up living for herself; and we children went to live with my grandfather, a tailor. After his death, and after many changes, we had a lodging, and there a sweep coaxed me with pudding one day, and encouraged me so well, that I didn't want to go back to my mother.

I was apprenticed to him on a month's trial, and I liked chimney sweeping for that month; but it was quite different when I was regularly signed up with him. I was cruelly treated then, and poorly fed, and had to turn out barefooted between three and four, many a morning in frost and snow. In first climbing the chimneys, a man stood beneath me, and pushed me up, telling me how to use my elbows and knees, and if I slipped, he was beneath me and caught me, and shoved me up again. The skin came off my knees and elbows – here's the marks now, you see.

I suffered a great deal, as well as Dan, a fellow-sweep to me, a boy that died. I ran away from my master once but was caught and taken back, and was rather better used. My master then got me knee- and

This sketch was made from a photograph, and shows one of the very few 'climbing sweeps' who still worked in London in 1850. (After that time, most sweeps used expanding brushes instead, like the ones on page 48.) You can see the short brush that he is carrying on his left arm, and the soot scraper he holds in his right hand.

ankle-pads, and bathed my limbs in salt and water, and I managed to drag on seven sorrowful years with him.

Then I was glad to be my own man at last, and I cut loose from the sweep trade, bought pipes to play, and started with an organ man, as his mate. I saved money with the organ man and then bought a drum. He gave me five shillings a week and my food, drink, washing and lodging. But now times are changed, and all for the worse for me. **99**

APPRENTICE Most skilled Victorian tradesmen – from chimney sweeps to plumbers and butchers – employed boys and young men to learn the business while they worked at the job. An apprentice was bound to stay with his employer for a certain period of time, and they received training as well as their board and keep and perhaps also a small wage. The apprentices expected to qualify in the trade at the end of that period. Some trades still run apprenticeship schemes today.

"We've nothing else to do"
Henry Mayhew: Mudlarks in the Thames

Mudlark boys roam about the sides of the Thames river at low tide, picking up coals, bits of iron, rope, bones, and copper nails that fall while a ship is being repaired. They are at work sometimes early in the morning, and sometimes late in the afternoon, according to the tides.

Mudlark scavengers had the very worst jobs of all in Victorian London. The work was filthy and dangerous, and paid very little money, so you had to be desperate to take it on.

They usually work from six to seven hours per day. My informant, a quick, intelligent little fellow, who has been at the business three years, tells me the reason they take to mudlarking. Their clothes are too bad to look for anything better, and they are nearly all fatherless and their mothers are too poor to keep them. So they take to mudlarking because they have nothing else to do.

This boy works with about twenty to thirty mudlarks every day, starting at daybreak very often, groping about, and picking out the pieces of coal from the mud. They go into the river up to their knees, and in searching the mud they often run pieces of glass and long nails into their feet. When this is the case they go home and dress the wounds but must return directly, for should the tide come up without their finding anything, they must starve that day.

At first it is a difficult matter to stand in the mud. My informant told me that many young beginners fall in. The coals he finds, he sells to the poor people in the neighbourhood at a penny the 'pot' (about 14 pounds in weight). The iron, bones, rope and copper nails he sells to the rag shops. They often pick up tools such as saws and hammers in the mud; these they either give to seamen in exchange for biscuits and beef, or sell to the shops for a few halfpence.

The mudlarks earn from about threepence a day. After they leave the river they go home and make themselves as tidy as possible, and then go into the streets and make a little money by holding gentlemen's horses, or by opening cab doors for the gentry. In the evening they go to the ragged schools, if they can.

The boy I spoke to keeps his sick mother, who cannot work, by mudlarking. His sister helps by selling fish. The poor little fellow owes five shillings in rent. He has a suit of clothes and a pair of boots in pawn for four shillings – and if he could get them out of the pawnshop he could find some better employment.

RAGGED SCHOOLS were set up to provide a basic education for poor children, before there was a national education system. They were usually run by volunteers who employed the teachers and sometimes taught the children themselves. The Ragged School Union was a national organization with the Earl of Shaftesbury as its chairman. The Union later became the Shaftesbury Society, and is still a charity today.

THE PAWNSHOP Poor people in Victorian times often pawned whatever they could to get money for food, or to pay rent. They tried to reclaim their possessions when they had saved some more money. Some families went through the same process week after week as they battled to make ends meet.

"A daily battle with the rising river"
James Greenwood 1867

A ragged coat buttoned over a shirtless back, a wonderful collection of materials fashioned to the shape of trousers to the knees. A pair of brown muddy legs beneath, renewed at every tide, completes the costume of the mudlark. We never saw a lark without one which is invariably used as a handy receptacle for the rags, bones and other offal that fall their way. How the larks came by their name is a mystery.

No matter the weather – blazing July or bleak December – there they are as sure as the retreating tide. The same old faces in the same squalid rags, from seven to seventy, raking their daily bread from the filthy shore of the Thames. Gaunt children, brawny men, tottering old women: each may be seen daily battling with the rising river for a crust.

Great storms and sudden floods are the mudlarks' harvest times – and it is not only the Thames that provides this. When the usually black and sluggish Fleet ditch bursts its bounds, it crushes and carries away the floorings of cellars and underground dwellings, and engulfs the squalid furniture of the wretched dwellers. Clamorous men and women in boats surround the mouth of the great sewer, watching for the goods as they emerge from over the massive iron door that guards the entrance. Legless tables, broken chairs, fragments of bedsteads, butchers' blocks, beams from underground slaughterhouses – all heaped in confusion in the boiling river.

For weeks after such an event mudlarks drop from the top of the gate into the slush below and wade, feeling through the pitchy darkness, groping with their feet as they go for anything sunk to the bottom in the tenacious mud.

THE FLEET RIVER ran through London from the north, and joined the Thames in the east, near Clerkenwell. Over the years it became a dirty sluggish ditch, and had been covered over by the time this article was written. The Fleet river is remembered in London place names (like Fleet Street) and still exists today, deep underground.

"We know full well it's all wrong"
Thomas Archer: Homeless children

The most terrible sight in London is its homeless children. Ride homewards on your omnibus in summer time and you may see some of them turning Catherine Wheels [cartwheels] in the dusty roadway, and running till they are mere quivering heaps of tatters, on the chance of a penny. Going up the silent highway of the Thames on board a steamer, you have noted them wallowing in the slime and ooze of the river shore. They shout to you to 'Chuck a copper!' and then dive for it in the mud. Plashing along the streets on a wet night, you have heard their bare blue feet patter on the stones for the chance of risking sudden death by opening the door of a cab.

They start up suddenly at street-corners or from the pale glare of the lamps outside a tavern-door, or emerge from the cellar-flap of a gaudy gin shop. They fight for orange peel, or cigar ends, or the nameless refuse that may be found about theatres. They startle you with their plaintive wheedling as you pause at the entrance of deserted streets. They come upon you suddenly from under the wheels of vehicles, with outstretched hands, asking you to buy cigar lights, or to 'Remember the sweeper!' whose useless broom stump is his only stock-in-trade. Some of these miserable little rogues grin under the brim of a man's hat or assume a long-tailed coat, worn as an incentive to passengers who may give for fun what they would never concede to famine.

In this phase of their wretched lives we all know them, and think of them sometimes with pity, pretending to hope that it is all right, but knowing full well that it is all wrong. It is only when they have nothing to sell, and dare not beg, and are driven like vermin to their holes, where they lie shuddering in the wet and cold, dreaming those wild dreams of food that visit the starving, that we do not see them. Few know that awful side of their existence: the side that they themselves, with the shy instinct of the hunted and the hungry, hide from the eyes of society, and sometimes die without revealing.

This little match girl sold boxes of matches on the London streets, calling 'A box o' matches, sir: two hundred and fifty wax-'uns for a penny!' or 'Two boxes of flamers, the best a-going.' Victorian matches were called 'lucifers' and contained yellow phosphorus, which was a deadly poison. Harmless red phosphorus later replaced it, and even today match-heads are often still coloured red, for that reason.

STREET ENTERTAINMENT

The Victorians invented the whole idea of leisure time. Before the Victorian era and the rise of industry there were no weekends off, and no special time allocated for rest and play. But when industrial workers had cash in their hands and a little time for themselves, theatres and music halls flourished as never before. The Victorian versions of mass media – such as printing and photography and even the first pop songs and pop stars – emerged as well. The poor on London's streets could benefit too, even though they probably couldn't afford tickets for a show. The streets were filled with casual entertainers of every kind – dancers and acrobats, musicians playing instruments and singing the popular ballads of the day, and animals performing tricks. There were few books; no television or radio; no CDs or computer games; yet everyone could enjoy some form of entertainment.

⟻ PERFORMERS & DANCERS ⟻

Alfred Rosling Bennett: Street performers

In the 1920s, Alfred Rosling Bennett wrote down his memories of the street performers he had seen in London, as a child, 60 and 70 years before.

The Raree show
This was a box supported on a stick or a barrow, in which were placed pictures (sometimes rude paintings) which could be viewed through peepholes, on payment of a halfpenny. The box was often surmounted by the Union Jack and by placards announcing the rarity and beauty of the pictures within; with perhaps an earnest entreaty to 'support the Fine Arts'. Some boxes were lighted at night by a candle and people (chiefly children) were attracted, sometimes by sound of a trumpet. During the Crimean War and Indian Mutiny the Raree shows were very popular, but after 1860 the Raree show died in London. Its pictures were poor, and it was a sorry business. Yet the arrival of such a show in a country village was still quite an event earlier in the century.

Glass blowing
A glass-blowing exhibition figured amongst the street entertainments of the 1860s. At a portable stall a tallish man (in a tall hat, of course) with a blow-pipe and several small pots of melted glass, probably heated by charcoal, produced globes and various small glass articles in different colours, which he sold to admiring

crowds. He was particularly expert in evolving masses of iridescent glass fibre, which he called silk, and for which customers never lacked.

Jack in the Green
Jack in the Green was produced occasionally by amateurs, and appeared only on May 1st, known as Chimney Sweeps' Day. (Chimneys took care of themselves on this anniversary, and if any unluckily caught alight they had to burn without the sweep's help to put them out, or have the Fire Brigade.)

After breakfast the sweep, with wife, family and friends sallied forth. The sweep was covered with a circular wicker frame like a beehive, which reached from a dome above his head down to his boots, with a small window to see through. This frame was entirely concealed by green boughs and flowers. Women and girls, one to each corner, and two or three men or youths, sometimes with sooty faces, mouth organs and tambourines, escorted this figure, and the women wore short dresses, white stockings and gaudy shoes, like May Queens. The sweep pranced, twirled, jumped and capered to music while the others danced around him. The public gave generously to the Jack in the Green shows. In a residential street, almost every house sent a maid or a child out with something for them.

Oyster grottoes
Oysters were cheap in the nineteenth century, and very popular with ordinary people. They were sold at four for a penny from costermongers' barrows and improvised corner stalls – already opened, and sprinkled with vinegar and pepper. Oyster consumption in London

streets ran into many millions, and this produced a lot of shells. In turn, the free availability of shells inspired children to produce Oyster grottoes. At the beginning of the oyster season, boys and girls collected the shells and built in any convenient street corner or recess a sort of domed temple. After dark, a lighted candle-stump was placed inside it, and imaginative youngsters made windows with bits of coloured glass or tinsel, and often produced a pretty effect. The children then stood by their grottoes and earnestly invited wayfarers to 'remember the grotto', which a good many of them did, with ha'pennies.

Puppet shows
Punch and Judy was an ever-popular show. The puppeteer was usually accompanied by a comrade who usually wore a white hat, had a mouth organ stuck in his stock or neckerchief, and carried a drum. The noise of these instruments was very familiar, and children a street or two off could tell when a Punch and Judy show was nearby. The comrade musician also acted as a collector of money, but later on this was done by a youth or woman who looked after the ha'pence and did nothing more.

Sometimes there was a show of dancing puppets that used the Punch-style portable stage, with let-down curtains to conceal the operator. Female figures performed a ballet of four or six, and a sailor danced the hornpipe; but the most exciting piece was a skeleton puppet, that danced alone. For a time the skeleton's whole frame danced, but then his bones began to separate and, marvellous to relate, disappeared behind the scenes, dancing all the time. At last, when the skull alone was left – still footing it merrily – the fragments

PUNCH · AND · JUDY

HAVE you a penny? well then, stay!
Haven't you any? don't go away!
Punch holds receptions all through the day,
Squeaking aloud to gather a crowd,
Scolding at Toby, beating his Wife,
Frightening the Constable out of his life,
And making jokes in a terrible passion,
As is Mr. Punch's peculiar fashion;
For this is his old, delightful plan
Of getting as many pence as he can.
    Then away he'll jog,
        With his Wife and his Dog,
        New folks to meet
        In the very next street.

An illustration from an 1880 children's magazine shows what a Punch & Judy show of the time may have looked like. The Punch and dog puppets are up on stage so the puppeteer must already be hidden behind the curtains. His assistant bangs the drum to attract an audience, and later he'll collect money from them.

returned one by one and reunited themselves, each in its proper place. Then the skeleton, finding itself all there and quite itself again, ended the performance with a graceful bow!

"Punch's season is holiday time"
Henry Mayhew: The Punch & Judy man

The performer of Punch was a short, dark man, dressed in a greasy and very shiny green jacket. This was fastened by one button in front, all the other buttonholes having been burst through. He had formerly been a gentleman's servant, and was especially civil in his manners. He came to me with his hair tidily brushed for the occasion, and was very communicative. He took great delight in talking like Punch while some young children were in the room, and who looked all about for Punch when they heard the familiar voice.

❝I am the proprietor of a Punch's show. I go about with it myself, and perform behind the green baize. I have a partner to play the music, and I've been five and twenty year now at the business. I wish I'd never seen it, though it's been a money-making business – the best of all the street exhibitions.

I was a footman in service and I had £20 a year and my board and lodging, and two suits of clothes. But a young man told me I could make a pound a day at the Punch and Judy business, after a little practice. And the gentleman I worked for went back to France to live and I was five months out of employment, living first on my wages and then on my clothes, until all was gone but the few rags on my back. So I began to think that the Punch and Judy business was better than starving. I should think any thing better than that – though it's a business that, after you've once took to, never can get out of. The boys will never leave me alone till I die, I know; and I suppose in my old age I shall have to take to the parish broom. I don't know a Punch's showman that hasn't died in the workhouse. Something else might turn up, to be sure – we can't tell the luck of the world.

Punch is a dramatic performance, a play, you may say. There are tragic parts, and comical sentimental parts, too. But when I first started I couldn't play the drum and pipes, so the young man did that himself, to call the people together before he got into the show. I used to stand outside, and patter to the figures. There was not much talk required then; merely calling out the names of the puppets as they came up, and these my master prompted me with from inside the frame. The first time I made my appearance I collected eight shillings, and after the performance my master said, 'You'll do!'

I kept on with my master for two years, and saved enough to start a show of my own. I gave 35 shillings for the stand, and 12 figures and the other things such as the ladder, horse, bell, and stuffed dog. The heads of the characters were all carved in wood, and dressed in the proper costumes. A good show at the present time will cost three pounds for the stand alone including baize, the frontispiece, the back scene, the cottage, and the letter cloth, or what is called the drop scene at the theatres.

The great difficulty in performing Punch consists in the speaking, which is done by a whistle in the mouth, called a call. I was six months in perfecting myself in the use of it. I kept practising away night and morning with it until I got it quite perfect. It was no use trying at home, because it sounds quite different in the open air. When I was practising I used to go into the parks and fields and out-of-the-way places, so as to get to know how to use it.

I have a partner to play the drum and pipes, and collect the money. My wife used to stand and keep the boys from peeping through the baize whilst I was performing behind it, and she used to collect the money afterwards as well, but she's been dead five years. In older times we used to go about with a trumpet, but now only Her Majesty's Mail may blow trumpets in the streets.

We start on our rounds at nine in the morning, and remain out till dark at night. The best hours for Punch are in the morning from nine till ten, because then the young children are at home. After that, they go out with the maids for a walk. From twelve till three is good again, and, then, from six till nine, because the children are mostly at home then, too. We in general walk from twelve to twenty mile every day, and carry the show, which weighs a good half-hundredweight at least. Speaking all day through the 'call' is very trying, especially when we are chirruping up so as to bring the children to the windows.

Monday is the best day for street business but Friday is no day at all, because the poor people have spent all their money. We do much better in the spring than at any time in the year, excepting holiday time at Midsummer and Christmas. That's what we calls Punch's season. We do most at evening parties in the

A showman sets up a puppet show stage in 1842, while his assistant blows a bugle to bring people from the surrounding streets. You can see the curtains that will hide the puppeteer, wrapped around the top of the poles.

holiday time, and if there's a pin to choose between them, I should say Christmas holidays are the best. For attending evening parties now we generally get one pound and our refreshments – as much as they like to give us – but the business gets slacker and slacker every season. Where I went to ten parties twenty years ago, I don't go to two now. Everybody looks at their money now before they part with it, and haggle and cheapen us down to shillings and sixpences.

We do best in wet weather. It looks like rain this evening, and I'm uncommon glad of it, to be sure. The wet keeps the children indoors all day, and then they want something to quiet them a bit, and the mothers and fathers, to pacify the dears, give us an order to perform. It mustn't rain cats and dogs – that's as bad as none at all! What we like is a regular good steady Scotch mist, for then we take double what we do on other days. In summer we do little or nothing; the children are out all day enjoying themselves in the parks.

Boys are the greatest nuisance we have to contend with. Wherever we go we are sure of plenty of boys for an audience – but they've got no money and they'll follow us for miles, so we're often compelled to go miles to avoid them. Wherever we know the children swarm, those are the spots we make a point of avoiding. Why, the boys are such an obstruction to our performance that often we're obliged to drop the curtain for them. They'll throw one another's caps into the frame while I'm inside it, and do what we will we can't keep them from poking their fingers through the baize and making holes to peep through.

Soldiers again we don't like, they've got no money – not even so much as pockets. Nurses aren't good either. Even if the mothers of the dear little children have given them a penny to spend, the nurses take it and keep it for ribbons. **99**

Henry Mayhew: The Guy Fawkes man

Gentlefolks pray, remember this day!
'Tis with kind notice we bring
The figure of sly and villainous Guy,
Who wanted to murder the king.
By powder and store he bitterly swore,
The parliament too, by him and his crew
Should all be blowed up in the air.

66I'm in the crockery line, going about with a basket and jugs and glass and that, but for the last eight years I have, every fifth of November, gone out with a Guy.

I was a nineteen-year-old when I first went out with a Guy. I said, 'It ain't no good doing as the others do, we must have a tip-topper.' It represented Guy Fawkes in black velvet. It was about nine feet high, and he was standing upright with matches in one hand and lantern in the other. It was the first big one that was ever brought out, there had been paper ones as big, but never a one dressed up in the style mine was. I had a donkey and cart and we placed it against some cross rails and some bits of wood to keep him steady. The Guy must

This 1877 photograph shows an enormous Guy with a demon-like face. It is so heavy that it has to be wheeled through the streets of London on a donkey cart. The three attendants have taken a lot of trouble with their rather exotic costumes.

have cost a sovereign. He had a trunk hose and white legs, which we made out of a pair of white drawers, and yellow boots, which I bought in Petticoat Lane. We took over three pounds with him which was pretty fair, and just put us on again, for November is a bad time for most street trades, and getting a few shillings all at once makes it all right till Christmas. **99**

Henry Mayhew: The street clown

He was a melancholy-looking man. I saw him performing in the street with a school of acrobats soon after I had been questioning him; and the readiness and businesslike way with which he resumed his professional buffoonery was remarkable. The tale he told proved that the life of a street clown is perhaps the most wretched of all existences. Jest as he may in the street, his life is literally no joke at home.

66I have been a Clown for sixteen years. I was left motherless at two years of age, and my father died when I was nine. His master took me as a stable boy, and I stayed with him until he failed in business. I was then left destitute again, and got employed at Astley's Theatre, and got an insight into theatrical life. I got acquainted, too, with singing people, and could sing a good song, and came out at last on my own account in the streets.

I've tried to get out; a friend advertised for me for any situation as groom, and I've tried to get into the police, and other things, but somehow there seems an

The clown in this engraving is a portrait of the unhappy one who talked to Henry Mayhew. His costume – which is described on page 74 – is a classic outfit for a clown. You can see the same sort of costume on some circus clowns today.

impossibility to get quit of the street business. Many times I have to play the Clown with a very heavy heart; you can't imagine what a curse the street business often becomes, with its insults and starvations. I dare say that no persons think more of their dignity than persons in my way of life. I would rather starve than ask for relief from the parish. Many a time I've gone to work without breakfast, and played Clown until I could raise a dinner.

I wear red striped cotton stockings, with full trunks, which are striped red and dotted red and black. The body, which is dotted like the trunks, fits tight, like a woman's gown, and has full sleeves and frills. The wig or scalp is made of horsehair, which is sown on to a white cap, and is in the shape of a cock's comb. My face is painted with dried white lead. I grease my skin first, and then dab the white paint on (flake white is too dear for us street clowns). After that I colour my cheeks and mouth with vermilion. I never dress at home. We all dress at public houses. In the street where I lodge only a very few know what I do for my living. My wife and I try to keep the business a secret from our neighbours. My wife does a little washing when able, and often works eight hours for sixpence. I go out at eight in the morning, and return at dark. My children hardly know what I do. They see my clown dresses lying about, but that is all. My eldest is a girl of thirteen. She has seen me dressed at the fair and she laughs when she sees me in my clown's dress, and wants to stay with me; but I would rather see her lay dead before me than she should ever belong to my profession.

Frequently, when I am playing the fool in the street, I feel very sad at heart. I can't help thinking of the bare cupboard at home; but what's that to the world? I've often and often been at home all day, when it's been wet, with no food at all, either to give my children or take myself, and have gone out at night to the public houses, to sing a comic song and play the fool for a meal. And when I've come home I've called my children up from their beds, to share the loaf I had brought back with me. I know three or four more Clowns, as miserable and bad off as myself.

I know only of one other regular street Clown in London beside myself. Some schools of acrobats, to be sure, will have a comic character of some kind or other to amuse the people while the money is being collected; but these, in general, are not regular Clowns. They are mostly dressed and got up for the occasion. The street Clowns generally go out with dancers and tumblers. There are some street Clowns to be seen with the Jacks in the Greens, but they are mostly sweeps, who have hired their dress for two or three days. I think there are three regular Clowns in the metropolis, and one of these is not a professional: he never smelt the sawdust.

When I go out the first thing I do is a comic medley dance, and then after that I crack a few jokes, and that is the whole of my entertainment. The first part of the medley dance is called The Good St Anthony. Then I do a waltz, and wind up with a hornpipe. After that I go through a little burlesque business. The old jokes always go the best with our audiences. The older the better, for the streets.

Most of the street Clowns die in the workhouses. In their old age they are generally very wretched and poverty-stricken. I can't say what I expect will be the end of me. I daren't think of it. 🟊🟊

"It's harder than a blacksmith's work"
Henry Mayhew: The street dancers

It is about twelve years [the early 1840s] since dancing was introduced into the public streets as a source of entertainment. Before that time the lower order of dancers were confined to the travelling booths. The first dancer who made his appearance in the streets did only the Sailor's Hornpipe, dressed in character. It was very successful then, and produced about nine or ten shillings on a fine day. The success of the first street dancer soon spread and they are always performed on a small piece of board (about three feet long and two feet wide), placed in the middle of the road. The most popular dances are the Sailor's Hornpipe, the Lancashire Clog Dance, the Highland Fling, and a comic medley dance.

"It is thought to be easy work – but I find it to be much harder than even a blacksmith's work, which was the business I was brought up to. It strains the nerves of the legs and sinews, and is more tiring than the sledgehammer. I was at smith's work five years, and got upon an average from fifteen shillings to a pound a week when I followed it. But I thought I could do better at dancing, and so I did at first; though now I don't make a quarter of what I did at my trade, and have picked up habits that have quite unsettled me. Ah, I was young when I left it, and now I begin to see my folly. Had I stuck to my trade it would have been a good thing for me and my poor wife. I'd go to anything indeed rather than be as I am. Our life is so uncertain. There is no Saturday night you know, sir. You get your money in dribs and drabs, and being about we are obliged to drop into public houses, and so a good part of even the little we do get goes in beer. We are obliged to have beer at the publics where we go and dress.

I used to dance to my fellow workmen of a night, and was thought a little of; that was why I took to it. Occasionally two dancers will join, one doing the Highland Fling and another the Sailor's Hornpipe. And sometimes one will go out alone with a Clown, or a Billy Barlow, and then they all share equally. A small party generally does better than a large one. The wives of the street dancers are generally very poverty stricken, and very miserable. Some do a little needlework or washing, but many are dependent solely upon their husbands' exertions, and often they have neither food nor fire at home. **99**

"I may dance half an hour for a ha'penny"
Henry Mayhew: The old soldier

Among the street dancers or performers is a soldier who dances with considerable spirit and gesticulation. His appearance is that of an ordinary foot soldier, well sunburnt. His dress is an artilleryman's blue jacket, and a pair of (patched, but clean) grey trousers, with a dark blue military cap.

"My jacket is not what I might be entitled to wear by right of my military service, but it was given to me at the barracks, by soldiers who had a feeling for a comrade. The lodging-house where I live is of the better kind; only adults are admitted. I couldn't bear to live in a house where there were boys and girls, and all sorts – there's such carryings on.

My father was a carpenter, but I followed no trade. I think I could have given my mind to trade; but I don't know, for I wasn't tried, and I always thought of a soldier's life and a roving one too. I used to look into the barracks to see the soldiers, and I thought a soldier's life was a fine life; but God knows it isn't. I served in Spain three years before I went to India, and I marched 100 miles barefoot over the hills and through the desert in India. I suffered a good deal in forced marches with just a reasonable amount to eat, but the water was the worst.

When I was discharged in the Himalayan mountains I came down the Ganges river (three months of it in boats) to Calcutta. When I got back to London and to India House, on my return here, I received three shillings – that's all. I kicked up a row at India House for some employment, and was taken before the Lord Mayor, who sent me to prison because I was turned into the streets to starve. I was ill three months after that, and was in the Free Hospital, ill of fever and want.

I had to beg with matches, and met with all kinds of insult and contempt, till I thought dancing was better than begging, with a turn every now and then in prison for begging, for I never stole in my life. I was nervous the first time I tried dancing but now I dance anything that comes into my head. It pleases the people; they like the

The old soldier told Mayhew that he served in northern India, and was discharged from army service in the Himalayas. He probably fought in the harsh deserts and mountains of what is now Afghanistan, like the soldiers in this painting during the Anglo-Afghan War of 1842.

soldiers; they say, 'This poor man works hard, he deserves a halfpenny, and he sells a few books, we'll buy one.'

I always do it in the uniform. I reckon one shilling is a very good day's work but oftener get eight-pence or nine-pence. It's hard work, killing work. I may dance half an hour, too, for a halfpenny and break my old boots to pieces. I would like to get out of this, I'm heartbroken and footsore, for I walk from twenty to thirty miles every day, except Sunday, besides being hunted by the police to stop my gathering a crowd. I never did eat idle bread in my life, and would do anything for an honest living. **"**

"Oh! Oh! Tragedy oh!"
Henry Mayhew: Billy Barlow

This is a comic character that accompanies the street dancers or acrobats. His costume is a cocked hat and red feather, a soldier's coat, white trousers with the bottoms tucked into Wellington boots, a large tin eyeglass, and an old broken and ragged umbrella. The nose and cheeks are coloured bright red with vermilion. The 'comic business' consists of the song called 'Billy Barlow' together with a few old conundrums and jokes, and sometimes a comic dance as well.

"I go about now as Billy Barlow. The character of Billy Barlow was originally played at the races, by a man who is now dead. He was about ten years at the street business doing nothing else than Billy Barlow in the public thoroughfares, and at fairs and races. He might have made a fortune had he took care on it, sir, but he was a great drunkard, and spent all he got in gin. He died seven years ago where most of the street performers end their days – in the workhouse.

The song of Billy Barlow (which was very popular then) was among the lot that he sung, and that gave his name. He used to sing, too, the song of 'I hope I don't intrude', and for that he dressed up as with this old umbrella, the eyeglass, and the white trousers tucked into the boots, all part of the costume at present. Another of his songs was 'Merry month of May, or follow the drum' and for that he put on the soldier's coat and cocked hat and feather which I wear to this day.

I have been for thirty years at the street business, off and on. I was a muffin and biscuit baker by trade, but I got fond of a roving life. My uncle was a performer at Covent Garden, and when I was nine years old I was one of the devils that danced around him in 'Mother Goose'. When I was fourteen years old my uncle apprenticed me to the muffin business, and I stuck to it for five years, but when I was out of my time I made up my mind to take to performing. First I played Clown at a booth, for I had always a taste for the comic, and after that I took to play the drum and pipes, and since then I have been chiefly performing as musician to different street exhibitions. When business is bad in the winter or wet weather, I make sweetmeats and go about the streets and sell them. I never made muffins since I left the business – you see I've no stove or shop for that, and never had the means of raising them.

I've done much the same since I took to the Billy Barlow, as I did before at the street business. We all share alike, and that's what I did as the drum and pipes. I never dress at home: but my wife knows the part I play. She came to see me once, and laughed at me fit to bust. I sneak my things out, and dresses at a public house. Joking is not natural to me, and I'm a steady man; it's only in the way of business, and I leave it on one side when I've got my private apparel on. I never think of my public character if I can help it until I get my show dress on. I'm glad to get it off at night, and then I think of my home and children, and I struggle hard for them, and feel disgust at having been a Tom Fool to street fools. **"**

Billy Barlow

Oh ladies and gentlemen how do you do?
I've come out before you with one boot and shoe,
I do not know how 'tis, but somehow 'tis so,
Oh! Isn't it hard upon Billy Barlow.

Oh! Oh! Tragedy oh!
Now isn't it hard upon Billy Barlow.

⇒ ANIMAL SHOWS ⇐

Alfred Rosling Bennett: Street performers

The Happy Family

Another Victorian street exhibition I remember was the Happy Family, and they were all somewhat similar. They consisted of a large wire cage occupying half of a hand barrow, the rest being boarded over to provide a stage for the performers.

The content of the cage was not constant, varying with the tastes of the proprietor and, no doubt, with the availability of specimens. But it nearly always contained a dog, two cats, half a dozen mice of sorts, several canaries or finches, and, occasionally, a small monkey. The initial wonder was to see creatures so antagonistic by nature occupying the same apartment in apparent harmony.

The performance would commence by opening the cage door and calling the cats by the names of famous boxers. They came out, had miniature boxing gloves put on their paws, stood on their hind legs, and pretended to box. After a time the man would ask the dog 'if he didn't see the family fighting?' The dog would bark a reply, and, charging out of the cage, come between the combatants to separate them. Having stopped the fight he retired, wagging his tail. Then the cats would perform again, and were once more stopped by the dog. In the end a medal was hung round the neck of one cat and a bandage tied round one eye of the other, and they were told to sit at two corners of the platform. Then, almost under the cats' noses, the mice walked a tightrope carrying balancing-poles. A bird fired a toy cannon, and another, affecting to be killed, permitted itself to be placed in a coffin and towed away on a hearse without a sign of life till the carriage stopped at the cage door, when it revived and hopped in. The supposed murderer was executed by placing his head

The Happy Family

HERE'S my Happy Family,
Little folks, as you may see:
Cats who fight, but just in fun,
Mice who up the flag-staff run,
Paroquet, canaries too,—

Now, my dears, 'twixt me and you,
Girls and boys who scold and tease,
Might a lesson learn from these
Birds and beasts who all agree
In my Happy Family.

Like the picture on page 67, this was drawn for a children's magazine by Thomas Crane (brother of the famous artist Walter Crane). The boy on the right is probably meant to be a coster, but everyone is too clean and well dressed to be street children.

in a running noose, suspended from a gibbet, which another bird tightened by pulling. Then the showman, after going around the crowd with the cap for money, sought another pitch. The public always provided a crowd, although there was a notion abroad that such effects could only be produced by ill-treatment of the animals. Whether the police deemed these displays obstructive or the Society for the Prevention of Cruelty to Animals intervened I don't know, but Happy Families grew scarcer and scarcer. The last I saw was on the Thames Embankment by Charing Cross Bridge some time in the 1880s.

THE SOCIETY FOR THE PREVENTION OF CRUELTY TO ANIMALS was formed in Britain in 1824, and became the Royal Society (the RSPCA) in 1835. Later in the century a law was passed banning cruelty to animals – the first such law in the world. Victorian ideas about the rights and welfare of animals, however, were very different from modern ones. A show like 'Happy Families' described above, or the 'Bird & Mice Show' below, could not be licensed or performed today.

"Much admired by people of taste!"
Henry Mayhew: The bird & mice show

❝I perform with birds and mice, in the open air, if needful. I was brought up to juggling by my family and friends, but colds and heats brought on rheumatism, and I left juggling for another branch of the profession; but I juggle a little still.

My birds are nearly all canaries, a score of them sometimes, and I have names for them all. I have Mr and Mrs Caudle, dressed in character; they quarrel at times, and that's self-taught with them. Mrs Caudle is not noisy, and is quite amusing; they ride out in a chariot drawn by another bird, a goldfinch 'mule', he harnesses himself up to a little wire harness. Mr and Mrs Caudle and the mule are very much admired. Then I have Marshal Ney in full uniform, and he fires a cannon to keep up the character. I have a little canary called The Trumpeter, who jumps on to a trumpet when I sound it, and remains there until I've done. Another canary goes up a pole, as if climbing for a leg of mutton, or any prize at the top, as they do at fairs, and when he gets to the top he answers me. He climbs fair, toe and heel, no props to help him along. These are the principal birds, and they all play by the word of command, and with the greatest satisfaction and ease to themselves.

I use two things to train them – kindness and patience; and neither of these two things must be stinted. The grand difficulty is to get them to perform in the open air without flying away, when they've no tie upon them. I lost one by its taking flight at Ramsgate, and another at Margate. They don't and can't do anything to teach one another; not in the least; every bird is on its own account; seeing another bird do a trick is no good whatever. I teach them all myself, beginning with them from the nest. I breed most of them myself.

To teach them to sing at the word of command is very difficult. I whistle to the bird to make it sing, and then when it sings I feed, and pet, and fondle it, until it

A street entertainer with three performing dogs, and a monkey, which has been taught to ride on the back of a dog. You can see the drum slung on the entertainer's back, ready to attract people's attention when his show is about to start.

gets to sing without my whistling, understanding my motions. Harshness wouldn't educate any bird whatsoever. I pursue the same system all through.

The bird used to jump to be fed on the trumpet, and got used to the sound. To train Marshal Ney to fire his cannon, I first put the cannon like a perch, for the bird to fly to for his food – it's fired by stuff attached to the touch-hole that explodes when touched. The bird was frightened before he got used to gunpowder, but after a few times he didn't mind it.

I train mice too, and my mice fetch and carry like dogs, and three of them dance the tightrope on their hind legs, with balance-poles in their mouths. They are hard to train, but I have a secret way, found out by myself, to educate them properly. They require great care, and are, if anything, more difficult than the birds. I have no particular names for the mice; they are all fancy mice, white or coloured. Ladies and children are my best friends generally, and my shows are very much admired by people of taste. **99**

MARSHAL NEY was one of Napoleon's generals when the British defeated the French at the Battle of Waterloo in 1815.

⤜ ACROBATS & JUGGLERS ⤛

Alfred Rosling Bennett: Street performers

Acrobats and jugglers

Acrobats and jugglers (who were usually called tumblers) frequently occupied pitches at convenient street corners. One troupe visiting our neighbourhood was made up of an elderly man, a youth and a girl – possibly all of one family. They spread a carpet, opened a box of properties, threw off their coats and appeared in regulation acrobatic dress. A basin for the collection of money was at one corner of the carpet.

The old man performed feats of strength and dexterity, and the others aided him. His chief act – and it was one common to most of the street tumblers – was to support and balance a pole about ten feet long vertically in his waistband, and then to allow the youth to climb to the top, and there go through several tricks. To keep the balance he had to watch the pole narrowly, hands on hips, as it shifted, but I never witnessed a failure. Then he would take both boy and girl on his shoulders, where they would posture and disport in various ways. He would fasten a cup to his forehead by a band, and, throwing a gilded ball high in the air, catch it in the cup every time. And he would keep half a dozen balls rotating, and so on. This, with crowded traffic of all kinds circulating within a few feet, required nerve and self-possession. I don't know how many pitches they made in a day, but the old man must have been a tough one to stand the racket.

You can see these acrobats have put down a mat on the cobbled street, but it must still have been an uncomfortable surface for the man on the ground. There are some juggling balls in the background, to use for another trick.

"What's the use of wishing?"
Henry Mayhew: The acrobat

An acrobat explains his profession.

❝The acrobats are generally tumblers or posturers. A tumbler is one who throws somersaults, headsprings, lion's leaps, and such like. A posturer is a man who puts his leg behind his head, or does what we call 'the frog', namely, he puts his two legs over his shoulders, and hops along on his hands.

The bending tumbler is one who can bend his head back down to his feet and pick up a sixpence, or such like. We have a man with our school whose body seems all joints and bendable everywhere. He fairly sits on his own head, bringing it down his back, his chin resting on the ground, and he looks out from between the top of his thighs.

A juggler I consider a man who balances plates, throws balls, and feats of that kind; whereas a conjuror is a man who performs tricks of deception by sleight-of-hand, changing cards, coins, and so on.

I should like to emigrate to Australia, where I could get on by perseverance, for I have plenty of that. I wouldn't be an acrobat there, of course, but a labourer of some description. I should like it, but cannot even get on to the first step of the ladder. My wife also wishes to emigrate; but what's the use of such people as us wishing?❞

"Toy shops are the ruin of us"
Henry Mayhew: The juggler & conjuror

The following account of a street juggler's business came from a grave-looking man, of dignified appearance both in face and figure, and with long well-oiled locks of hair got up expressly for public display.

❝I have been twenty-eight years in the profession of a juggler. I was a plasterer born, as the saying is, but family circumstances, such as I'd rather not state, led me to form a connection with old Mr Saunders, and with Saunders' company I juggled on stilts, both in town and country. I believe no man in England but me ever juggled on stilts five feet high.

When I started first I did well – most excellent, and never knew what it was to want money. I dare say I made my five pounds every week when I began. I performed on the stilts, with brass balls (from one to five), throwing them up and down and catching them – like an Indian juggler, only he juggles from the ground, and I on my stilts. After the brass balls I threw large brass rings, catching them, and then linking them together. Then I threw three large daggers, or rather from one to three (I have thrown more) all round about my body, catching them as they came. I next took a wooden pole, and on the top of it a wash hand basin – the pole was seven feet high. And on the top of the pole, still on my stilts, I kept the basin spinning round.

I kept to the stilts until six or seven years ago, doing pretty well. After the stilts I performed on the ground, and now I carry a small box which stands on four legs,

This juggler seems to be working the crowd alone, although he does have a drummer to attract an audience and collect the money. There are more juggling balls on the ground – perhaps he's going to try for six at once?

and with it I'm mostly to be seen. I perform out of doors as well as at parties. The box is to hold my apparatus. In one of my tricks I appear to eat a quantity of shavings, and draw them afterwards, in the shape of an immense long barber's pole, out of my mouth. A little doll I make appear and disappear from the folds of a cloak. I show the cloak to be empty, and the next moment there's the doll in it. The shavings, the pole, and the doll are generally called for, if I try anything else. These are my juggling feats.

As to conjuring, I do all sorts of things with cards. I make them do anything but speak. I do chiefly the old tricks such as the shavings, which are not known in the toy shops – these toy shops, with their toy tricks, are the ruin of us. I teach conjuring and juggling but I have no pupils – worse luck. I've taught many an amateur conjuror, real gentlemen, who amuse their friends that way; some of them take to it very kindly, and I make them perfect conjurors if I can. I had a natural turn for the profession myself, and didn't require teaching. I perfected myself by study and practice. There are, I believe, only eight persons whom I can rank with myself as regular professional men in London; but toy shops send out their own conjurors now, and the number of chance conjurors – and they are half gamblers many of them – is uncertain. I don't reckon them professionals.

This time of the year is the best of my seasons, but I can make nothing like what I used to make. I've been ill too, or else I might make my two pounds a week or even more, bad as it is. The wintertime is my slack time, except about Christmas. I juggled at Vauxhall in 1831, before the Queen. I find town the best for me, but common hands do best in the country; the people are not up to the town mark there. **99**

"Begin before your bones are set"
Henry Mayhew: An adult tumbler

❝I have been in this business since I was two years of age. My father was in the profession, and was my teacher. I tumbled at two years old, and have followed it until now, which is twenty-six years. I was made to tumble when a child, but my father wasn't cruel to me. He took up the trade of tumbling; he had been a soldier, a silversmith, and a shoemaker, before he became a tumbler.

We must begin tumbling young, before the bones get set. At two years I used to bend back and pick up pins with my eyes – four pins – and then drop them one by one. I do that still. It wasn't very painful to learn this, but I had the headache often, and my nose used to bleed. I used to tremble a good deal when doing it as a child, and I still do now, if I leave it off and begin it again.

As I grew up I learned other tricks. I can stand on my head, and walk round my head with my legs, while I keep my head standing still. That required a great deal of practice to get perfect – two months perhaps – when I was seven or eight years old. It's a laborious thing, but not painful. I can walk along on my elbows, with my legs over my head; it's not painful to me, but it would be to others. I learned that when I was twelve or thirteen.

I have been in this trade all my life, and a very bad trade it is. Some days I may take sixpence or a shilling or sometimes one shilling and sixpence. The best day's work I ever had was ten shillings, but it's all casual and depends greatly on the weather. On a fine day like this I might make seven or eight shillings in the street, with luck, but on wet days I can do nothing but the public houses, and public-house work is very bad indeed. In summer the nights are very short, and night's the only time for tavern tumbling. In one public house I was stooping back to pick up the pins with my eyelids, and a fellow, half drunk, kicked me, and the pins stuck about my eyes, and it's a mercy I wasn't blinded. I've had gin flung in my eyes, and snuff, and have been subjected to every kind of insult, perhaps for no money at all, when I've performed in a public house.

The street's the best for money, but there the boys heave stones at you and the policemen order you on, and go you must. Gentlefolk, both male and female, are my best patrons; the ladies are best generally. Country is generally better than town for me, but only in summer. I find my own dresses, which come expensive. My dress is made of elastic cotton; it costs me seven shillings, and it lasts only six or seven weeks. In bending and tumbling it's strained all to pieces. Tumbling strains every nerve in the body as well as the dress. I ought to know what it does, for I can manage all these tricks – I can walk on my hands and jump on my hands, put a penny under my toe, bend back and pick it up with my mouth without putting my hands to the ground, and bend my body back and pick up four pins with my eyes. I can do lion's leaps – that's to jump over chairs like a cat, pitching on my hands and going on; I can bend backwards and bring my head and feet into a tea saucer; do head springs, or go on my head and turn over without using my hands. That's about all. I can't tell which trick is most admired, for I do them all at one performance, leaving the walking round my head to the last.

I am very strong in the back, and in the muscles of my leg and thigh, but I have never tried all my strength. I want to get out of this line of life, and get into shoemaking, of which I do know a little. To know how to make shoes well is better than all the tricks I know, for the profession is very bad. I owe a man ten shillings for giving me instructions in making children's shoes, and I'm improving very much in the trade. If I had children, I wouldn't like to bring them up to be tumblers. 99

This portable organ is almost as large as a piano, and it has attracted a crowd of people in this London street. The musician (in the cloth cap) is getting ready to play, and the little girls in pinafores look eager to dance to the music. The photograph was taken in the 1890s.

≈ MUSICIANS ≈

Alfred Rosling Bennett: Street performers

Musicians

I remember one man who played (or made a noise on) five or six instruments at once. He had a drum on his back struck by a stick tied to the elbow; cymbals on his knee played by a string from the foot; bells on his head that jangled when he shook it; a mouth organ; an accordion, and so on.

The Highland pipers had not arrived in London at that time, but there was a Tyrolean bagpiper who played a dozen bars of the same tune incessantly, all day and every day. There were Italians with hurdy-gurdies and white mice, marmots or squirrels in rotating cages. The hurdy-gurdy was a squeaky instrument that operated by the friction of a wheel against a violin string.

There were two tribes of organ grinders. One used a tall-backed instrument which tinkled, was played by a crooked handle at one end. The other was a wind-and-reed affair in a rectangular box and was much fuller in tone. Both kinds of organ grinders were carried on the back, and supported on sticks when performed on. The square box of the second kind often served as stage for a monkey, gaudily attired, which was forced to dance or to go through a few tricks.

A marrow-bone-and-cleaver band

One amateur turn I recall was the marrow-bone-and-cleaver band. As a rule, this came to life only in honour of a butcher's wedding, when he and his bride were serenaded by apprentices and boys belonging to the butcher's craft. Some tapped together two bones in castanet fashion, while others clashed big bones against cleavers. They produced a strong rhythm, but never a tune. Complaints were made when such musicians went through the streets at night!

Playing the bells
Other entertainers carried frames that were hung with an octave or two of small bells, and produced sweet music. One of these troupes had a piebald pony which played 'Home, Sweet Home' and other simple melodies, by striking the bells with his right hoof. Once I had the luck to find out how it was done, when the screen behind the bell frame got disarranged one day and I peeped inside. There stood a man who, while his mate was out in front patting the pony and chatting to the crowd, pointed with a whip at each bell to be struck. The pony, seated on its haunches, could see the hidden man and faithfully followed the lead, chiming out several tunes.

"Playing four accordions with my feet"
Henry Mayhew: The bell & accordion player

❝I have been blind since within a month of my birth and have been twenty-three years a street performer. My parents were poor, but they managed to have me taught music. I was one of a street band in my youth, and could make fifteen shillings a week at it.

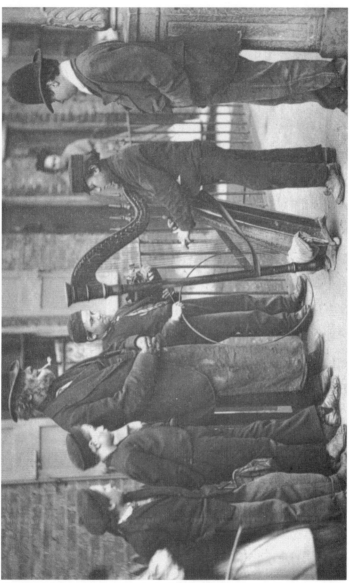

The audience for this young harpist includes some working people – you can see a long apron on the bearded man, for instance, which suggests he is a carrier. On the other hand, the boy with a hoop has probably come out to play with it, and has stopped to listen to the harp. The photograph was taken in 1877.

But I didn't like the band, for if you are steady yourself, you can't get others to be steady, and so no good can be done.

I started the bells I play now, as near as I can recollect, some eighteen years ago. When I first played them I had my fourteen bells arranged on a rail, and tapped them with my two leather hammers held in my hands in the usual way. Then I thought I could introduce some novelty into the performance. The novelty I speak of was to play the violin with the bells. I had hammers fixed on a rail, so that each bell had its particular hammer, connected with cords to a pedal, and so by playing the pedal with my feet, I had full command of the bells. I made them accompany the violin, so that I could give any tune almost with the power of a band. It was always my delight in my leisure moments, to study improvements such as I have described.

I played the violin with my feet also, on a plan of my own and the violin in my hand. I had the violin on a frame on the ground, arranged so that I could move the bow with my foot in harmony with the violin in my hands. The last thing I have introduced is playing four accordions with my feet. The accordions are fixed in a frame, and I make them accompany the violin. Of all my plans, the bells and violin did the best, and are the best still for a standard. I can only average twelve shillings a week through the year, which is very little for two people, for I must have my stepson to lead me about. **" "**

Henry Mayhew: Blind musicians

Most street musicians obtain their money by agreeable performances. The blind musicians, however, do not use music to please their listeners, but as a means of getting their attention. They have their regular rounds to make, and particular houses at which to call on certain days of the week, and are mostly well-known characters. Many of them have been performing in the streets of London for years.

"They call me Mrs Tuesday"
Henry Mayhew: The hurdy-gurdy woman

She is clean and very tidily dressed, and accompanied by her usual attendant in the streets, who was almost as clean and tidy as herself. Her countenance is cheerful, and her manners those of a well-contented old woman. She plays on an old hurdy-gurdy, which she calls a cymbal. It has a battered, heavy look with it, and is grievously harsh and out of tune. She has been about the streets of London for about forty years, and being blind has always needed a guide. Her cheerfulness, considering her poverty and the precarious mode of her life, was extraordinary. Her attention to her guide was most marked. If a cup of tea was given to her after her day's rounds, she would be sure to turn to the poor creature who led her about, and ask, 'You comfortable, Liza?' or 'Is your tea to your liking, Liza?'

She rode in a cab for the first time to go and have her photograph taken, and her fear at being pulled backwards (for she sat with her back to the horse) was almost painful. She felt about for something to lay hold of, and did not appear comfortable until she had a firm grasp of the pocket. In a short time, however, she began to enjoy the ride. 'Very nice, isn't it Liza?' she said to her guide, who accompanied her. 'But I shouldn't like to ride on the steamboats, they say they're dangerous; and as for the railways, I've heard tell they're dreadful; but these cabs, Liza, are very nice.' On the road she was continually asking where they were, and wondering at the speed at which they travelled. 'Ah!' she said, laughing, 'if I had one of these here cabs, my rounds would soon be over.'

66I was born the 4th April, 1786 (it was Good Friday that year) at a small chandler's shop, facing the White Horse in Drury Lane. Father was a hatter, and mother was an artificial-flower maker and feather finisher. When I was but a day old, the nurse took me out of the warm bed and carried me to the window, to show some people how like I was to my father. The cold flew to my eyes and I caught inflammation in them. My eyes were then very bad, by all accounts, and owing to mother being forced to be from home all day at her work, I was put out to a nurse when I was three weeks old. My eyes were then very bad, by all accounts, and some neighbours told the woman I was with that Turner's Cerate would do them good. She got some and put it on my eyes, and from that time I never did see afterwards. She did it, poor woman, for the best; it was no fault of hers, and I'm sure I bear her no malice for it.

This engraving was made from a photograph of the hurdy-gurdy woman whose story begins on the opposite page. Her companion, Eliza, is with her. Hurdy-gurdies, like the one she holds, are still made and played by folk musicians.

I stayed at home with mother until I was thirteen, when I was put to the Blind School, but they turned me out because I was not clever with my hands, and I could not learn to spin. I had not been used at home to do anything for myself – not even to dress myself. Mother was always out at her work, so she could not teach me, and no one else would, so that's why I was turned out. I then went back to my mother, and when she died I was just sixteen. Father died too, seven weeks after Mother, and when they had both gone I felt I had lost my only friends, and that I was all alone in the world and blind. But, take it altogether, the world has been very good to me, and I have much to thank God for and the good woman I am with. I missed Mother the most, she was so kind to me; there was no one like her; no, not even father.

The parish paid for my learning the cymbal; God bless them for it, I say. A poor woman in the workhouse first asked me to learn music; she said it would always be a bit of bread for me; I did as she told me, and I thank her to this day for it. It took me just five months to learn the cymbal (if you please – the hurdy-gurdy isn't its right name). The first tune I ever played was 'God save the King,' well, it's the Queen now. 'Oh, Susannah!' I learnt myself by hearing it on the organ. I always try and listen to a new tune when I am in the street, and get it off if I can: it's my bread after all.

The woman who persuaded me to learn the cymbal took me out with her; I lived with her, and she led me about the streets. When she died I took her daughter for my guide. She walked with me for more than five-and-twenty year, and she might have been with me to this day, but she took to drinking and killed herself with it. She behaved very bad to me at last, for as soon as we got a few halfpence she used to go into the public and spend it all; and many a time I'm sure she's been too tipsy to take me home. It was very cruel of her to treat me so, but, poor creature, she's gone, and I forgive her I'm sure. I'd many guides after her, but none of them was honest like Liza is: I don't think she'd rob me of a farthing, would you, Liza?

I've my regular rounds, and I've kept to them for near upon fifty year. All the children like to hear me coming along, for I always play my cymbal as I go. At Kentish Town they call me Mrs Tuesday, and at Kensington I'm Mrs Friday, and so on. The cymbal isn't hard to play; the only thing is, you must be very particular that the works is covered up, or the halfpence is apt to drop in.

We're very tired by night time; aren't we, Liza? But when I get home the good woman I lodge with has always a bit of something for me to eat with my cup of tea. She's a good soul, and keeps me tidy and clean. I help her all I can; when I come in, I carry her a pail of water upstairs, and such-like. Many ladies that have known me since they were children allow me a trifle. One maiden lady has given me sixpence a week for many a year, and another allows me eighteen pence a fortnight; so that, one way and another, I am very comfortable, and I've much to be thankful for.

OH, SUSANNAH!

I come from Alabama
With my banjo on my knee
I'm going to Louisiana,
My true love for to see.
It rained all night
The day I left
The weather it was dry
The sun so hot,
I froze to death
Susannah, don't you cry.

Oh, Susannah!
Oh don't you cry for me
For I come from Alabama
With my banjo on my knee.

I had a dream the other night
When everything was still
I thought I saw Susannah
A-coming down the hill.

Oh, Susannah!
Oh don't you cry for me
For I come from Alabama
With my banjo on my knee.

This is one of the songs the hurdy-gurdy woman performed. It was written
by Stephen Foster, an American, in 1847.

"I'm not a great performer"
Henry Mayhew: A blind woman violinist

I had the following narrative from a stout, blind woman, dressed in a clean cotton gown, the pattern of which was almost washed out. She was led by a very fine dog (a Scottish collie, she described it), a chain being attached to the dog's collar. A boy, poor and destitute, barefoot and wearing a greasy ragged jacket, with his bare skin showing through many rents, accompanied her; the boy had been with her a month, she supporting him.

❝I have been blind twelve years. I was a servant in my youth, and in 1824 married a journeyman cabinet-maker. I went blind from an inflammation two years before my husband died. We had five children, all dead now – the last died six years ago; and at my husband's death I was left almost destitute. I used to sell a few laces in the street, but couldn't clear two shillings and sixpence a week by it. I had a little help from the parish, but very rarely.

A neighbour, a tradesman, then taught me to play the violin, but I'm not a great performer. I wish I was. I began to play in the streets five years ago. I get halfpennies for charity, not for my music. Some days I pick up two shillings, some days only sixpence, and on wet days, nothing. I've often had to pledge my fiddle at the pawnshop for two shillings – I could never get more on it, and sometimes not that. When my fiddle was in pledge I used to sell matches and laces in the streets, and had to borrow money to lay in a stock of them.

My chief places when I've only the dog to lead me are Regent Street and Portland Place, and really, people are very kind and careful in guiding and directing me – even cabmen, may God bless them. **99**

Alfred Rosling Bennett: Street performers

Ballad singers

The ballad singers were very good at making the most of dramatic news such as gruesome murders or executions. They were always present and prepared with a woeful ballad written to suit the crime. But in our neighbourhood the ballad singer was most often visible on Saturday evenings, when he planted a wooden frame – sometimes it was a clothes horse – covered with ballads hung on horizontal strings, at street corners, and attracted a crowd by singing some well-known song with force and emphasis. He sold copies of the words printed on long strips of coarse paper at a halfpenny or a penny, I forget which, and never lacked custom. The popular songs of the 1850s were often set to simple melodies that had plenty of 'go', and stuck to the memory. Many of them ended with a nonsensical chorus of 'Fol de-lol' or 'Doodledum-day', but that practice was dying out. Words and music were both picturesque, and bursting with enthusiasm.

Long-song sellers sold the words of popular songs of the day, which were printed on long strips of paper. The clothes this long-song seller is wearing make him look quite prosperous, although they are probably second-hand.

"It's the tune that makes the ballad!"
Henry Mayhew: Song sellers

Some pin up the songs on a board or wall where they stand to offer their books of songs, or individual sheets of separate songs; others sing the songs they offer for sale.

"In a proper ballad on a subject there's often twelve verses, none of them under eight lines, and there's a four-line chorus to every verse, and if it's the right sort, it'll sell the ballad. It's not the words that ever make a ballad though; it's the subject – and more than the subject it's the chorus, and far more than either, it's the tune!**"**

"The farmyard on a fiddle"
Henry Mayhew: The animal-noises fiddler

"I imitate all the animals of the farmyard on my fiddle. I imitate the bull, the calf, the dog, the cock, the hen when she's laid an egg, the peacock, and the ass. I have done this in the streets for nearly twelve years.

I was brought up as a musician at my own desire. When a young man (I am now 53) I used to go out to play at parties, doing middling until my sight failed me. I then did the farmyard on the fiddle for a living. Though I had never heard of such a thing before, by constant practice I made myself perfect. I studied from nature. I never was in a farmyard in my life, but I went and listened to the poultry anywhere in town that I could find them, and I then imitated them on my instrument.

The Smithfield cattle gave me the study for the bull and the calf. My peacock I got at the Belvedere Gardens in Islington. The ass is common, and so is the dog, and them I studied anywhere. It took me not more than a month to acquire what I thought a sufficient skill, and then I started it in the streets. It was liked the very first time I tried it.

I never say what animal I am going to give. I leave that to the judgement of the listeners; and they can always tell. I can make twelve shillings a week this year, and I play it in public houses as well as in the streets. My pitches are all over London, and working people are my best friends. **"**

⇒ PHOTOGRAPHY ⇐

The invention of photography in the mid-nineteenth century created a tool as powerful and important as the printing press. It changed people's ideas of history, of time, and of themselves. It also changed their ideas about privacy, because cameras could record most areas of human life.

A cartoon from *Punch* magazine in the 1860s:
Old lady (who is not used to such new-fangled notions as photography): 'Oh Sir! Please sir! Don't sir! Don't for goodness' sake fire, sir!'

Most of the street photographers whose stories and advertisements follow probably used a photographic process called collodion, which had been made public in 1851. Collodion photography was fast and produced pin-sharp detail. But the process was a complicated one, and took skill to manage. It was difficult to achieve good results, especially when photographers were working in tents in the street.

Other photographic processes of the time included daguerreotypes and ambrotypes. Some photographers also specialized in creating multiple copies of a single image. These were trimmed and mounted, and sold as visiting cards. By the end of the nineteenth century many households had family photograph albums. Some also collected stereoscope cards, which created 3-D illusions.

DAGUERREOTYPES: Before digital cameras were invented, photographs were made from positive or negative images of the subjects. The first photographs were daguerreotypes (named after Louis Daguerre, the man who invented the process). Daguerreotypes were produced from positive images on polished metal plates, fixed permanently in place by light-sensitive chemicals. The photographic process called collodion started with negative images on glass plates. The images were fixed permanently to the glass with a chemical called collodion. Ambrotypes used collodion negative images, which were bleached and backed with black paper.

An out-of-doors photography session in 1877. Anyone who wanted a photograph taken had to sit completely still in the chair beside the developing cart while the plates were exposed. It looks as though the baby's parents are waiting to bring him into position for a photo – baby carriage and all!

Henry Mayhew: Sixpenny portraits

Within the last few years photographic portraits have become a regular article of street commerce. In the West End of London people have little idea of the number of persons who gain a livelihood by street photography. There may be one or two photography galleries that supply shilling portraits. But in the eastern and southern districts of London, such as in Bermondsey and the Whitechapel Road, one cannot walk fifty yards without passing some photographic establishment, where for sixpence persons can have their portrait taken, and framed and glazed as well.

It was in Bermondsey that I met a street photographer taking sixpenny portraits in a booth built up out of old canvas, and erected on a piece of spare ground in a furniture-broker's yard. Into this yard he had driven his yellow caravan, where it stood like an enormous Noah's Ark. In front of the caravan, by means of clothes horses and posts, over which were spread out the large sail-like show cloths (used at fairs to decorate the fronts of booths) he had erected his operating room. This is only just tall enough to allow a not-particularly tall customer to stand up with his hat off. A glazed roof had been arranged for letting light into this little tent.

On the day of my visit the photographer was doing a large business, despite the cloudy state of the atmosphere. A crowd in front of his tent was admiring the photographic specimens, which, of all sizes and in all kinds of frames, were stuck up against the canvas. Inside the operating room a crowd of women and children was assembled, all waiting their turn to be taken. The photographer remarked, as I entered, that when one girl comes for her portrait, there's a dozen comes along with her to see it done.

The portraits were taken by the photographer's wife. She, with the sleeves of her dress tucked up to the elbows, was pointing the camera at a lady and her little boy. From the little boy's wild and nervous expression, he seemed to think that she was taking her aim previous to shooting him! The photographer said that people preferred a woman to a man. 'Many's the time a lady tells us to send that man away, and let the missis come,' he said. 'It's quite natural,' he continued, 'for a lady don't mind taking her bonnet off and tucking up her hair or sticking a pin in here and there before another woman, but she would object before a man.'

After the portrait had been taken I found that the little square piece of glass on which it was impressed was scarcely larger than a visiting card, and this being handed over was carried into the caravan at the back, where the process was completed. I was invited to follow the lad to the dwelling on wheels. The outside of the caravan was very remarkable, and of that peculiar class of architecture which is a mixture of coach-and-ship building.

'So you've taken him at last,' said the proprietor, snatching the portrait from the boy's hand. 'Well, the eyes ain't no great things, but as it's the third attempt it must do.'

The portrait was one of those drab-looking portraits with a light background, where the figure rises from the bottom of the plate as straight as a post, in the cramped, nervous attitude of a patient in a dentist's chair.

Another establishment close by had originally formed part of a confectioner's shop selling penny ices and *bull's-eyes – for the name-board over 'Photographic Depot' was still the property of the confectioner, and the portraits displayed in the window were surmounted by an announcement of 'Ginger beer, one penny and two pennies'. At this establishment the portraits were taken in a little alley adjoining the premises, where the light was so dim that even the blanket hung up at the end of it looked black, from the deep shadows cast by the walls.*

Here, a customer was persuaded to pay twopence to have the theory of photography explained to him. The salesman's lecture was to the effect, that the brass tube of the camera was filled with clockwork, which carried the image from the lens to the ground glass at the back. To give proof of this, the camera was carried to the shop-door and a boy who was passing by was ordered to stand still for a minute.

'Now, then,' continued the salesman, 'look behind here; there's the image, you see.' And then, addressing the boy, he added, 'Just open your mouth, youngster.' When the lad did so, he asked, 'Are you looking down the young un's throat?' The customer nodding assent.

'Well, that's the way portraits are taken,' said the salesman.

"People don't know their own faces"
Henry Mayhew: A street photographer's story

A tout at the door was crying out 'Hi! Hi! Walk inside! Walk inside! Have your correct likeness took, frame and glass complete, and only sixpence!'

❝I've been at photographic-portrait taking since its commencement – that is to say, since they were taken cheap – two years this summer. I lodged in a room in Lambeth, and I used to take them in the back yard – a kind of garden. I took a blanket off the bed and used to tack it on a clothes horse. My mate used to hold it, if the wind was high, whilst I took the portrait.

The reason why I took to photographing was, I thought I should like it better than busking with a banjo. I didn't know anything about photographs then, not a mite, but I saved up my money and got a loan of three pounds, and managed to get a complete apparatus for taking pictures and opened the next day. I never knew anything about taking portraits then, though they showed me when I bought the apparatus (but that was as good as nothing, for it takes months to learn). The very next day when I had the camera, I got a customer before I had even tried it out. So I tried it on him, but I didn't know how to make the portrait, and it was all black when I took the glass out. I told him that it should come out bright as it dried, and he went away quite delighted. The first Sunday after we had opened I took one pound five shillings and sixpence, and everybody was quite pleased with their spotted and black pictures, for we still told them they would come out as they dried. But the next week they brought them back to be changed. By then I could do them better, and they had middling pictures – I picked it up very quick.

When I bought my camera at Fleming's the owner took a portrait of me with it to show me how to use it, and as it was a dull afternoon he took 90 seconds to produce the picture. So, you see, when I went to work

I thought I ought to let my pictures go the same time; and hang me if I didn't, whether the sun was shining or not. I let my plates stop 90 seconds, and of course they used to come out overdone and quite white, and as the evening grew darker they came better. When I got a good one I was surprised, and that picture went miles to be shown about. Then I formed an idea that I'd made a miscalculation as to my time, and by referring to the sixpenny book of instructions I saw my mistake, and by the next Sunday I was very much improved, and by a month I could take a very tidy picture.

Sunday is the best day for shilling portraits; in fact, the majority is shilling ones, because then, you see, people have got their wages, and don't mind spending. Nobody knows about men's ways better than we do. The largest amount I've taken at Southwark on a Sunday is over four pounds' worth, but then in the week days it's different; some days only three or four shillings.

We are obliged to resort to all sort of dodges to make sixpenny portraits pay. I always take the portrait on a shilling size; and after they are done, I show them what they can have for a shilling, the full size, with the knees; and table and a vase on it, and let them understand that for sixpence they have all the background and legs cut off. So as many take the shilling portraits as sixpenny ones.

Another of our dodges is the brightening solution, which is nothing more than aqua distilled, or pure water. When we take a portrait, Jim, my mate, takes it and finishes it up, drying it and putting it up in its frame. Then he wraps it up in a large piece of paper, so that it will take some time to unroll it, at the same time crying out to me, 'Take sixpence from this lady, if you please.' Sometimes she says, 'Oh let me see it first;' but he always answers, 'Money first, if you please ma'am; pay for it first, and then you can do what you like with it. Here, take sixpence from this lady.' When she sees it, if it is a black one, she'll say, 'Why this ain't like me; there's no picture at all.' Then Jim tells her that if she likes to have it passed through the brightening solution, it come out lighter in an hour or two. They in general agree to have it brightened; and so then, before their face, we just dip it into some water. We then dry it off and replace it in the frame, wrap it up carefully, and tell them not to expose it to the air, and in an hour or two it will be all right. Sometimes they brings them back the next day, and says, 'It's not dried out as you told us;' and then we take another portrait, and charge them more.

If the eyes in a portrait are not seen, and they complain, we take a pin and dot them; and that brings the eye out. If the hair, too, is not visible we takes the pin again, and soon puts in a beautiful head of hair. It requires a deal of nerve to do it; but in the end they generally go off contented and happy. Once a sailor came in, and as he was in haste, I shoved on to him the picture of a carpenter who was to call in the afternoon for his portrait. The jacket was dark, but there was a white waistcoat; still I persuaded him that his blue Guernsey had come up very light, and he was so pleased that he gave us ninepence instead of sixpence. The fact is, people don t know their own faces. Half of 'em have never looked in a glass half a dozen times in their life, and directly they see a pair of eyes and a nose, they fancy they are their own.**"**

Photographic studio advertisements

DAGUERREOTYPE OR

PHOTOGRAPHIC PORTAITS

PORTRAITS BY MR. CLAUDET'S INSTANTANEOUS PROCESS UNDER THE PATRONAGE OF HER MAJESTY, ARE TAKEN DAILY AT THE ADELAIDE GALLERY, LOWTHER ARCADE, STRAND.

The Sitting generally occupies less than One Second, by which faithful and pleasing Likenesses are obtained, with backgrounds, the patented invention of MR. CLAUDET, representing Landscapes, the Interior of a Library, &c. &c.

Price of a Single Portrait, usual size, One Guinea. Portraits and Groups are also taken on Plates of an enlarged size, and for Lockets or Brooches as small as may be required.

LIKENESSES. Have no more bad Portraits!
CAUTION!!!
All Persons are respectfully cautioned against the
many SPURIOUS IMITATORS OF THE ART
OF PHOTOGRAPHY,
Who not possessing the requisite knowledge
of Chemicals, CANNOT ENSURE A Correct
& Lasting Portrait!!

The consequence is, that thousands are dissatisfied with
the Portraits, although they have paid High Prices for them.

This evil can be entirely avoided by coming to
MR & MRS C. TIMMS, PRACTICAL
PHOTOGRAPHIC ARTISTS,
41, Newington Causeway.

Who are always at home to take portraits; the
certainty of your being pleased is, you are requested
not to pay until you are quite satisfied.

Many years' experience has proved to him that a
tradesman's success is commensurate with his
honesty, he is therefore most desirous of gaining the
gradually increasing confidence of the Public, than to
excite a temporary influx of Customers at the expense of
Truth. All Portraits are taken on the Ground Floor, so that
the aged are not necessitated to ascend flights of
stairs. It is particularly necessary to observe the Name
above the Door. C. Timms, 41, Newington Causeway.

An immense stock of Gold and Bird's-eye Maple
Frames to select from, also Best Silk Velvet, Fancy
Morocco Cases, Lockets and Brooches made expressly
for portraits. ESTABLISHED TWELVE YEARS.

NB. The Waterloo Omnibuses bring you from the Station to the
Elephant & Castle, when there, please enquire for TIMMS.

"Ducky darling, Henry Higgins!"
Strand *magazine, 1891: A day with an East End Photographer*

The stock-in-trade of an East end photographer is not a very elaborate one. He may pick up the whole apparatus second-hand for about £5 and the studio and fittings are not expensive. The thin metal plates cost not more than ten shillings a gross, and the frames about three shillings a gross. The chemicals amount to an infinitesimal sum on each plate. On a good day, a turnover of two to three pounds may be made. But there are many ups and downs and trials of temper and patience, to say nothing of the unhealthy nature of the business, all going to make up the disadvantages associated with the life of an East End photographer.

The tout outside the photographer's shop seemed to know the history of every person whose photograph was displayed in the showcase. He was rattling it all off to us when a slight diversion was created by a costermonger's barrow, drawn by a smart little pony, driving up to the front of the shop.

The driver was Mr Higgins, a costermonger, and the other occupants of the barrow were Mrs Higgins and their infant son and heir, Henry Higgins. Mrs Higgins had decided that her little Henry should have his photograph taken, and afterwards be glorified in a coloured enlargement. Mr Higgins had agreed to this being done, regardless of expense. It was a weighty responsibility for the photographer, who knew that photographing babies was not his strong point. But he reflected upon the increased fame to his business if he was successful, and he determined to do it or perish in the attempt.

It would have been hard to get enough light in this indoor photographic studio for a good photograph, although the pale sheet that hangs behind the woman and her child would have helped.

The photographer made hasty preparations by selecting the most tempting stick of toffee he could find, and the tout was instructed to buy a doll, a rattle, a penny trumpet from a neighbouring toy shop. The Higgins baby was duly placed in a chair, behind which Mrs Higgins was seated to keep the baby happy.

At first, Henry quietly sucked his thumb and surveyed the studio with an interested air, but as soon as he was encouraged to look at the photographer, a distrustful frown settled upon his face. His irritation at the photographer's presence found expression in a yell of infantile wrath. The more the photographer flourished the toys, the more the child yelled.

The photographer danced and sung, and blew the penny trumpet, but nothing worked. He was about to give up in despair, when he remembered the stick of toffee! This was produced, and had its effect. On being assured by his mother behind the chair that the 'ducky darling would have his toffee stick', the youthful sitter held that prospective joy with his tear-glistening eye.

The photographer at last performed the operation with a sigh of satisfaction. Baby Higgins had his toffee stick, Mrs Higgins had a pleasing photo of her infant offspring, and the photographer proudly congratulated himself on having so successfully performed his job.

Such is the life of an East End photographer. Today he may be doing a roaring business, but tomorrow he may be reduced to accepting the money of children who club together and demand that he take, 'Me, and Mary Ann, and little Mickey all for threepence'. He always agrees, for he knows that the photo will create a feeling of envy in the minds of other children who will decide on having a 'real tip topper' at sixpence.

⇒ NEWS, JOKES & GOSSIP ⇒

In modern Britain we can check on the latest news twenty-four hours a day, seven days a week. It isn't hard to learn about current events if you want to. The most interesting and important stories are constantly updated on radio and television, and on the Internet. Reporters and photographers fly around the world to comment on the latest international news and gossip, and their up-to-the-minute stories are transmitted into our homes.

It was very different in Victorian Britain. There were no telephones, radio, television or Internet. International news travelled very slowly. Even national news took hours, days or even weeks to spread throughout the country.

In the 1850s, when Mayhew interviewed people on the streets of London, newspapers and periodicals were the main source of entertainment, instruction, information and news. Most newspapers of the time were published every day, or at least several times a week. They were relatively expensive – about sevenpence a copy, which in today's money was worth something like four pounds. (When the *News of the World* was first published in 1843 it cost only threepence a copy, and newsagents at first refused to handle it at such a low price!) Only relatively rich people could afford a daily newspaper, and so they were mostly bought by upper-class and middle-class readers.

Periodicals [journals and magazines] were published less frequently than newspapers: they appeared only once a week, or every two or four weeks. Some of these – like *Punch* magazine, which Henry Mayhew helped to start – were intended for the same readers who could afford to buy quality newspapers. But there was also a constant demand

BLACK BESS
OR THE
Knight of the Road

'Black Bess, or the Knight of the Road' by Edward Viles was a popular serial story about highwaymen. The chapters were sold on the streets throughout the early 1860s, and were known as 'penny dreadfuls' because each chapter cost one penny. By the time the story was finished, it ran to more than 2,000 pages!

for cheap periodicals – the ones that were printed on unbound, loose sheets of paper and sold on street corners. These generally cost about one penny, or even less. Their subjects included topical ballads and romances, political satires and scandalous stories. A few of the better periodicals also published serial stories: some of Charles Dickens's novels were first published that way.

So it was periodicals, and not newspapers, that were the most popular sources of entertainment, and read by most people. Even street people knew about the periodicals. Some of the street sellers offered them for sale, and they were often shared around, and passed from hand to hand to save money.

"Thieves, highwaymen and pirates"
Henry Mayhew: A street seller of periodicals

❝I lost the use of this arm, ever since I was three months old. My mother died when I was ten and after that my father took up with another woman and turned me and my sister (she was two years younger than me) out into the streets. My sister got employment but I couldn't get work because of my crippled arm. I walked about, till I fell down in the streets for want.

At last a man, who had a sweetmeat shop, took pity on me. His wife made the sweetmeats and minded the shops while her husband went out juggling in the streets. He told me that if I would go around the country with him and sell a few prints while he was juggling in the public houses, he'd pay for my food and lodgings. I stayed with him for two or three years.

After that, I went to work for a waste-paper dealer. He'd buy up all the old back numbers of cheap periodicals and penny publications, and send me out with them to sell at a farthing a piece. He used to give me four pence out of every shilling, and I did very well with that. Sometimes I could make fifteen shillings on a Saturday night and a Sunday morning, selling odd tales like 'Lives of the Pirates' and 'Lives of the Highwaymen' – I've often sold as many as two thousand numbers on a Saturday night, and they were all about thieves and highwaymen and pirates. My main customers are young men. **99**

Riddles and conundrums

Riddles were sold as 'nuts to crack', and called conundrums, or enigmas. Here are some examples that were offered for sale on the streets of London in Mayhew's time.

**I'VE GOT NO WINGS, YET IN THE AIR
I OFTEN RISE AND FALL,
I'VE GOT NO FEET, YET CLOGS I WEAR,
AND SHOES, AND BOOTS, AND ALL.**

ANSWER: A FOOTBALL.

Question: How does a horse have ten legs?

Answer: A horse has two fore legs and two hind ones.
Two 'fores' are eight, and two more makes ten.

Question: How can you make the most of an opportunity?

Answer: Give a cabman the opportunity of working out his fare. You're sure to find that he will make the most of it.

My first is in tea but not in leaf
My second is in teapot and also in teeth
My third is in caddy but not in cosy
My fourth is in cup but not in rosy
My fifth is in herbal and also in health
My sixth is in peppermint and always in wealth
My last is in drink, so what can I be?
I'm there in a classroom, do you listen to me?

❖❖

THE SOLUTION IS TEACHER

Henry Mayhew: The running street patterer

The running street patterer announces the contents of the sheets of paper he is offering for sale, as he goes along the street. They usually claim to be selling the details of some gruesome and horrible murder, or of some extraordinary or exciting event that has aroused public attention. Continually on the move, they shout out a description of the contents of what they have to sell. It isn't often possible to hear exactly what the patterers call out as they run, but they make sure the public can hear key words such as: 'murder', 'horrible', 'barbarous', 'love', 'mysterious', 'former crimes', so as to attract buyers of their papers. Sometimes the papers turn out to be nothing to do with what was shouted – but by the time the buyers discover that, the patterer has run on.

"A good exciting murder"
Henry Mayhew: The standing street patterer

❝I have taken my five shillings, but paper-selling now isn't half so good as it used to be. People haven't got the money to lay out; for it all depends with the working man. The least we make in a day is upon an average sixpence; but taking the good and bad together, I should say we take about two shillings a day, or ten shillings a week. I know there's some get more than that, but then there's many take less.

People reckon me one of the best patterers in the trade. I'm reckoned to have the gift of the gab. But I never try a last dying speech on any other than the day of the execution – all the edge is taken off of it after that. The last dying speeches and executions are all printed the day before. They're always done on the Sunday, if the murderers are to be hung on the Monday. I've been and got them myself on the Sunday night, over and over again.

Gentlefolks, though, they won't have anything to do with murders sold in the street – they've got other ways of finding out about it. We lay on the horrors, and picture them in the highest colours we can. We don't care what's in the papers in our hands, all we want to do is to sell 'em; and the more horrible we make the affairs, the more sales we have.

I did very well with what I called 'The Burning of the House of Commons'. I happened by accident to put my pipe into my pocket amongst some of my papers, and burnt them. Then, not knowing how to get rid of them, I got a few straws. I told the people that my burnt papers were parliamentary documents that had been rescued from the flames, and that, as I dare not sell them, I would let them have a straw for a penny, and give them one of the papers. By this trick I got rid of my stock twice as fast, and got double the price that I should have done. (The papers had nothing at all to do with the House of Commons – we don't care what there is in the papers, so long as we can sell them.)

The chief things I work are quarter-sheets of recitations and dialogues. One is 'Good Advice to Young Men on Choosing their Wives'. I have done exceedingly well with that – it's a good moral thing. Another is 'A pack of cards turned into a Bible, a Prayer-book, and an almanac'. These cards belonged to a soldier, Richard Middleton, of the 60th Regiment of Foot, who was taken a prisoner for playing at cards in church during divine service. But the best I do is 'The remarkable dream of a young man of loose character'. The story is he had made an agreement to break into a gentleman's house, but owing to a little drink that he took he had a remarkable dream, and dreamt he was in hell. The dream had such influence on his mind that he refused to meet his comrade. His comrade was taken up for the burglary, found guilty and executed for it. This made such an impression on the young man's mind that he became a reformed character.

The papers that I work chiefly are what are called the standing patters. We can make most money of the murders while they last, but they don't last, and they merely want a good pair of lungs to get them off. But it's not everyone can work the standing patters. I believe there's only another man in London can do 'em beside me. It's too much for the common sort of flying stationers – it requires the gift of the gab. A man that's never been to school an hour can go and patter a dying speech or a battle between two ladies of fortune – they're what we call running patters – you're obliged to keep moving on with them. They require no scholarship at all. All you want is to stick a picture on your hat to attract attention, and to make all the noise you can – a good stout pair of lungs and plenty of impudence is all that is required.

I can assure you I often feel very nervous, it's just the same as a play actor. I begin it, and walk miles before I can get confidence in myself to make the attempt. Without confidence, you know, you can't do anything. I find that a foolish nonsensical thing will sell twice as fast as a good moral sentimental one; and, while it lasts, a good exciting murder will cut out the whole of them. **”**

A PACK OF CARDS TURNED INTO A BIBLE This story has lasted from at least the early nineteenth century to the present day, in many different forms. It appeared in books of recitations published in the early twentieth century, and was later adapted by country singers in the USA, as a song called 'The Deck of Cards'. In this, the soldier explains how he can use a deck of cards to remind him of the Christian Bible's teachings. The ace reminds him there is only one God; the two represents the two parts of the Bible, Old and New Testaments; the three represents the Father, the Son, and the Holy Spirit – and so on.

"A day in the life"
Charles Manby Smith: Charley Potter, the news boy

Ever since Tom Potter's death in a fall from scaffolding, to say nothing of the weary weeks he lay ill, it has been work or starve – do or die – with the rest of the Potter family. The widowed Mrs Potter took her oldest son Charley away from school. Charley was going on thirteen and as sharp a young fellow as need be, but now he must go out to work instead of his father. Charley was helped to employment from a newspaper agent, and

These competing newspaper sellers stand on the edge of the pavement in Ludgate Circus, east London, in 1893. Each one holds copies of their paper and flourishes a handbill to advertise exciting headlines. You can make out some of the headlines on the centre handbill, such as 'DEATH OF A FAMOUS ACTOR'.

while his mother Polly is at home washing or ironing, or abroad cleaning or nursing (with little Billy meantime taking care of the baby) we will follow Charley through the routine of one day's operation.

It is a dark, dreary, and foggy morning in January and the wind is driving from the south-east, bringing along with it a mixture of snow and rain. It is still two hours away from daylight when Charley, slinking from the side of his sleeping brother, turns out of bed and dons his clothes. He has no notion of washing his face just yet – that is a luxury which must be deferred till breakfast-time, which is a good way off.

The pelting sleet, the driving wind, and the fog are small trifles to Charley, and he takes no more notice of them than just to button his jacket to the chin, and lug his cloth cap down over his eyes, as he gently shuts the door after him, and steps out into the darkness. Then he digs his hands into his pockets, and bending his head towards the storm he steers round the steps of St Martin's Church, and then straight on along Fleet Street, where he disappears suddenly in the dark and narrow maw of Black Horse Alley. By daylight the alley is dark and unsavoury, and a black horse, or a horse of any colour, once in the alley, would find it a difficult matter to turn round, and would have to back out, or else, like an eel in a water-pipe, wait till destiny chose to release him. Wretched old tenements on either side shut out the daylight from the court, and one of these serves as a central newspaper depot. Whole tons of newspapers, received damp from the printing machine, take their departure daily from here, for all parts of Britain.

Here we must follow close upon Charley's heels. Diving into the court, we find the old house bathed in a flood of gaslight from top to bottom. Men and boys are rushing up and down the angular stairs, some with damp loads upon their backs, and others hastening off to get their own loads. The morning papers have all been 'put to bed', as it is termed, and their printing machines are now rolling off copies at the rate of several thousands an hour. As fast as they come they are counted off and borne away by the agents, and an enormous number come on the shoulders of newsboys to Black Horse Alley.

Charley is already at his work. He stands with a score of other lads and men, folding, packing, and bundling up papers in time for the morning train which will carry them to Bristol and to Birmingham, more than a hundred miles distant, and to a hundred places besides, in time for delivery before breakfast. All hands go at it together. As fast as one huge pile is cleared off, another comes, and neither the noise nor the activity relents until the well-filled bags are hoisted on young shoulders, or piled on light traps waiting close by in the street – and off they roll or run to the post office.

Charley staggers out of Black Horse Alley, looking, with a huge bag upon his shoulders, like a very great bird with a very small pair of legs. Once the papers are delivered to the post office the immediate hurry is over. But he must still make his way to the newspaper shop, where he meets half-a-dozen more boys – hired by the shopkeeper to deliver newspapers to local subscribers. The piles of newspapers are transferred from their swaddling blankets to the counter, rapidly sorted, and the boys start off on their missions. Charley's round ends a short distance of his own home, and so he can return there by nine o'clock.

With breakfast over, he gets back to the shop, where he finds a bundle of newspapers to sell at the railway station. Charley is off again – the bustle of trains arriving and departing excites his spirits and energies and, determined on doing business, he gives full scope to his lungs. 'Times,

In this sketch from 1871, boys like Charley Potter dash through busy London streets – dodging in and out of the traffic – to sell copies of their newspapers to omnibus passengers and pedestrians.

Times – *today's* Times! Morning Chronicle! Post! Advertiser! Illustrated News! *Who's for today's paper? Paper, gentlemen! News, news! Paper, paper, paper!* Chronicle! – *Who's for* Punch?' *In this way, he rings the changes backwards and forwards, not even pausing while engaged with a customer, and only holding his peace while the station is vacant. The arrival of a new batch of passengers wakes him up again, and he is among them in a moment, with the same incessant song and the same activity. His eyes are everywhere and he never loses a chance; he cherishes the first-class carriages especially, and a passenger cannot pop his head out of window for a moment, without being confronted with the damp sheet of* The Times, *and assailed with the ringing sound of his voice.*

Charley generally continues this until dinnertime at one o'clock. The newsboy's dinner is best described as an unknown quantity. It may consist of a warm and savoury stew at home with his mother, or it may be a crust of bread and cheese, eaten in the streets while hurrying back to the shop from the railway station. Sometimes he eats dinner and supper in one go, cheating his appetite with a hunch of bread and a cup of coffee; at other times, he will patronize the pie shops, and dine upon eel or mutton pies. But, dinner or no dinner, he must be at the newspaper shop early in the afternoon, to account for his sales and stock, and to help prepare for the evening mail trains.

All hands are busy in making up the big bag for the post office, which must be ready at the very latest, by ten minutes before six, the distance being fully a nine minutes' walk. There is the same ceremony with the evening papers as there was with the morning ones, and there is the same limit as to time for its performance. Before the race against the clock begins, Charley has the bag hoisted on his shoulders, and, with a fair couple of minutes to spare, is trudging steadily towards the post office.

Inside the broad area between the lofty pillars of the main post office wait a hundred or two of spectators, come to watch the rush of newspapers and letters, and policemen are in attendance to keep a clear passage, so that the very last arrivals shall meet no obstructions. As closing-time approaches, and the illuminated clock points to five minutes to six, the crowd increases. Sacks of all shapes and sizes, bulgy and slim, are seen walking up the stairs – some as long as bags of hops, beneath which the bearers stagger unsteadily towards the breach; others, of more moderate capacity, containing but a couple of bushels or so of damp sheets. All discharge their contents into the trapdoor near the entrance. The bags, as fast as they arrive, disappear through the trap and come flying out again empty. Here comes a monster-sack, borne by two men, which is with difficulty lugged into quarters, while others crowd after it, like a brood of chickens diving into the hole through a barn door after the mother hen.

Now is the critical moment.

The clock strikes, clang! In go a brace of bulky bags; clang! In go three more rolling one over another, and up rushes a lawyer's clerk, and darts forward to the letter box at the further corner, fencing his way with a long packet of red-taped foolscap, with which he makes a successful lunge at the slit.

Clang! Another brace of sacks have jumped down the throat of the post office, and more yet are seen and heard scrambling and puffing up the steps.

Clang! And in goes another bouncing bag, followed by a little one in its rear.

Clang! Nothing more. A pause and a general look of

inquiry: 'Is it all over?' No! Here comes another big bag dashing up the steps; in it rushes like mad!

Clang! Down falls the trapdoor. The exhibition is over, and the crowd disperse about their business.

It is a very rare occurrence for a bag of newspapers to arrive too late for the evening post. Newsboys have been known to carry their bags within very good time to what they consider a practicable distance, and then to wait for the first stroke of the bell – the signal for a headlong run over the remaining distance while the clock is striking. Sometimes this daring experiment is not successful, in which case the overconfident urchin has to return to the shop with his bag unloaded, to the consternation of his employer and his own disgrace. But Charley knows better than that. He has discharged his load among the first arrivals; and now his work is done for the day, and he strolls home.

There is a substantial supper waiting for him, which having well earned he has a right to enjoy, as he does enjoy it. After that, if the weather is dry, he will play with young Billy round the fountains in Trafalgar Square. If it is wet and cold, there will be a game with the baby before the fire; or if the baby should be asleep, Billy will get a writing lesson with slate and pencil; or spell out a column of last week's news. But Charley must be in bed early, because he must rise early again the next day. The boys are in bed when the bell of the neighbouring church rings out nine.

"Police! Police!"
A letter to The Times, *30 December 1861*

Sir,

We are exposed in this quarter of town to an intolerable nuisance. From 8 to 11 o'clock every evening a series of stentorian ruffians invade our quiet streets, shouting out at the top of their voices 'Second edition of the *Globe* – assassination of Lord John Russell!' or 'Third edition of the *Standard* – triumph of Major Beresford!' and so on. The papers they sell seldom contain a word connected with the startling news they proclaim, yet our children are affrighted from their slumbers and our invalids annoyed, so that the evening papers may sell a few additional copies.

Sweeps have been silenced; dustman's bells put down, monster organs suppressed. Why should we continue to suffer from this far greater nuisance?

I am Sir, your obedient servant,

A Belgravian

EATABLES AND DRINKABLES

In a city where ordinary working people seldom had kitchens of their own – and perhaps had nothing more to cook with than a kettle over an open fire – there was a lot of demand for cheap ready-made street food. Street markets flourished in every town. There were no supermarkets where you could buy food in bulk (and no refrigerators or freezers to keep it in) – so Victorians shopped more often, and ate more fresh food, than people do today. But they also ate a lot of stale or even rotten food – there were no food safety or hygiene laws to prevent that, and no sell-by dates and labels to watch out for.

Henry Mayhew: Eatables & drinkables

There are many varieties of street sellers. There are the street sellers of fish – wet (fresh) and dry (cured and smoked) fish, shellfish, and (from the same vendors) also poultry, game, and cheese. There are the sellers of vegetables and fruit (the fruit both green – fresh – and dried) who may also sell flowers, trees, shrubs, seeds, and roots, and 'green stuff' such as watercresses, chickweed and groundsel, and turf.

The street sellers of eatables and drinkables are also many and varied. They include vendors of fried fish, hot eels, pickled whelks, sheep's trotters, ham sandwiches, pea soup, hot green peas, penny pies, plum duff, meat puddings, baked potatoes, spice cakes, muffins and crumpets, Chelsea buns, sweetmeats, brandy balls, cough drops, and cheap meat for cats and dogs. Under the heading of street drinkables may also be specified tea and coffee, ginger beer, lemonade, hot wine, new milk from the cow, asses' milk, curds and whey, and (occasionally) water.

Henry Mayhew: A typical street boy's supper

He might begin with eels or pickled whelks, cold fried flounder, or periwinkles. Then would come the potatoes, apparently giving out so much steam that the can that contains them seems in momentary danger of blowing up. The potatoes are large, hot, mealy fellows; and he might next have a course of boiled feet of some animal or other, which he would be certain to find in front of the gin-shop.

There would be ginger beer from the fountain, at a penny a glass, or hot elder cordial as it was a cold night. For dessert he could calculate on all the delicacies of the season, from salads to baked apples, and none of these

Mayhew found that the baked potato trade was a profitable one in the colder months of the year. The potatoes were cooked in bake houses and then placed in cans like this one, where a fire pot filled with charcoal kept the potatoes hot. There is a small compartment for butter and salt at the far end.

things would cost more than a penny a piece; some of them would be under that sum.

There would be the digestive advantage of moving leisurely about from one course to another; and, above all, there would be no fee to waiters!

But of all these eating-stands, the chief favourite with a street boy is the potato can. They collect around it and there talk over local matters, or discuss the affairs of the adjacent cab stand. Sometimes they are joined by the watermen, whom they respect, more so perhaps than the policeman; certainly more than they do the street-keeper, for him they especially delight to annoy. They watch their fellows eating a potato with a curiosity and an attention most remarkable, as if no two persons fed in the same manner, and as if they expected something strange or diverting to happen at every mouthful.

STREET-KEEPERS were employed in some parts of London to limit the time and space in which people sold goods in the street. In Bethnal Green, for example, in east London, costermongers were not supposed to trade after 11.00 on Sunday mornings. Any costermongers whose barrows were still on the streets after that time could have them confiscated by the local street-keeper.

"Buttons and bugles, potatoes and periwinkles"
Richard Rowe: Leather Lane Market

A penny will buy a good many things in Leather Lane.

It will buy a glass of sherbet, or from three to four windfall oranges arranged in pyramids, and with skins as discoloured as more than a couple of the vendors' cheeks beneath the eyes; and here, where a constant tinkling is being kept up on an earthen pan, you can take your pick out of a box of stone-ware, 'all at one penny'.

'Mackerel all alive, all alive, oh! Fine silver mackerel, six a shilling,' shouts one coster. 'All a-blowing, all a-growing,' croaks his neighbour over his trap of flowering spring plants.

Eels and eggs; tin-pots and gown-pieces; crabs and combs; hardbake and bonnet-shapes. Dates conglomerated into a mass that looks as if it would need a hatchet to split it. Buttons, bugles, and other trimmings set out daintily on blue cards; potatoes and periwinkles; cabbages and coconuts, lemons and brass-tagged bootlaces. Boots and shoes, and beds and bedsteads; onions and old iron; plaice and photograph frames; radishes and rhubarb; and glass beads and bottles. Red herrings and money boxes; smoked haddocks and Dutch dolls; whelks, watercress, almond rock and apples, brass-headed nails and curious little slabs of bacon.

All these are only some of the things sold in Leather Lane.

"Who'll buy a bonnet for fourpence?"
Henry Mayhew: Saturday-night markets

The street sellers are to be seen in the greatest numbers at the London street markets on a Saturday night. Here, and in the shops immediately near the markets, the working classes generally purchase their Sunday's dinner. So after pay-time on Saturday night, or early on Sunday morning, the crowd in the New Cut, and such districts in particular, is almost impassable.

There are hundreds of stalls, and every stall has its one or two lights; either it is illuminated by the intense white light of the new self-generating gas lamp, or else it is brightened up by the red smoky flame of the old-fashioned grease lamp. One man shows off his yellow haddock with a candle stuck in a bundle of firewood; his neighbour makes a candlestick of a huge turnip and the tallow gutters over its side. Meanwhile, the boy shouting 'Eight a penny, stunning pears!' has rolled his dip in a thick coat of brown paper, that flares away with the candle.

Some stalls are crimson with the fire shining through the holes beneath the baked chestnut stove. Others have handsome lamps, while a few have a candle shining through a sieve. These, with the sparkling ground-glass globes of the tea-dealers' shops, and the butchers' gaslights streaming and fluttering in the wind, like flags of flame, pour forth such a flood of light, that at a distance the atmosphere immediately above the spot is as lurid as if the street were on fire.

The pavement and the road are crowded with purchasers and street sellers. The housewife in her thick shawl, with the market basket on her arm, walks slowly

These men have set up a street stall of 'fancy goods', which often included toffee and boiled sweets as well as handkerchiefs, reels of coloured thread, and pretty ribbons and buttons to decorate clothes.

on, *stopping first to look at the stall of caps, and then to try to beat down the price of a bunch of greens. Little boys, holding three or four onions in their hand, creep between the people, wriggling their way through every little space, and asking for custom in whining tones, as if seeking charity.*

Then the tumult of the thousand different cries of the eager dealers, all shouting at the top of their voices, at one and the same time, is almost bewildering. 'So-old again!' roars one. 'Chestnuts all hot, a penny a score!' bawls another. 'Buy, buy, buy, buy, buy – bu-u-uy!' cries the butcher. 'Half-quire of paper for a penny,' bellows the street stationer. 'An ha'penny a lot.' 'Tuppence a pound grapes.' 'Three a penny for Yarmouth bloaters [a smoked fish].' 'Who'll buy a bonnet for fourpence?' 'Pick 'em out cheap here! Three pair for a ha'penny, bootlaces.' 'Now's your time! Beautiful whelks, a penny a lot!' 'Come and look at 'em! Here's toasters!' bellows one with a Yarmouth bloater stuck on a toasting-fork. 'Penny the lot, fine russets,' calls the apple woman – and so the babble goes on.

One man stands with his red-edged mats hanging over his back and chest, like a herald's coat. The girl with her basket of walnuts lifts her brown-stained fingers to her mouth, as she screams, 'Fine warnuts! sixteen a penny, fine war-r-nuts.' A bootmaker has illuminated his shop-front with a line of gas, and in its full glare stands a blind beggar, his eyes turned up so as to show only the whites. He mumbles some rhymes that are drowned in the shrill notes of the bamboo-flute player next to him. The boy's sharp cry, the woman's cracked voice, the gruff, hoarse shout of the man, are all mingled together.

Henry Mayhew: Old street cries

There was a man who sold tripe, and his deep rich voice would ring through a whole street. 'Dog's-meat! Cat's-meat! Nice tripe! Neat's feet! Come buy my trotters!'

Then there was that delight of our childhood – the eight o'clock 'Hot spiced gingerbread! Hot spiced gingerbread! Buy my spiced gingerbread! Sm-o-o-king hot!'

Another very popular character among the boys, whose daily cry was: 'Hot spiced gingerbread nuts, nuts, nuts! If one'll warm you, wha-at'll a pound do? Wha-a-a-at'll a pound do?'

Henry Mayhew: The sweet stuff seller

"Boys and girls are my best customers, and mostly the smallest of them. But then again, some of them's turned fifty! An old fellow that hasn't a stump of a tooth in front, why, he'll stop and buy a halfpenny's worth of hardbake [toffee] and he'll say to me, 'I've a lot of the boy about me still,' though he doesn't show it anyhow, in his look. I'm sometimes thinking to introduce a softer sort of toffee – boiled treacle, some call it – just for old people that are 'still boys'. The old ones want something to suck, not to chew!"

Henry Mayhew: The scuttle-mouth oyster trade

In 1848, very large shelly oysters (the oyster meat inside being very small) were introduced from the Sussex coast. The costermongers called them by the name of 'scuttle-mouths', and at first their sale was enormous. One coster told me that on the Saturdays he not infrequently, with the help of a boy and a girl, cleared ten shillings by selling these oysters in the streets, disposing of four bags of them. (Reckoning twenty-one dozen to the bag he sold 2,016 oysters.) And as the price was two for a penny, he took just four pounds and four shillings by the sale of oysters in the streets, in one night.

With scuttle-mouth oysters, a costermonger takes no trouble. He throws them into a yard and dashes a few pails of water over them, and then places them on his barrow, or conveys them to his stall. Some of the better costermongers, however, lay down their oysters carefully, and give them oatmeal 'to fatten on' before they are sold.

In April last, some of the street sellers established oyster rounds. These were carried on by costermongers whose main business was over at twelve noon. They bought a bushel of scuttle-mouths (never another sort of oyster) and, in the afternoon, went around with them to poor neighbourhoods. Going these oyster rounds is hard work, I am told, and a boy is generally taken to assist. Monday afternoon is the best time for this trade, when ten shillings is sometimes taken, and four or five shillings' profit made.

THE OYSTER STALL.
"Penny a lot, Oysters! Penny a lot!"
[From a Photograph.]

Oysters were a cheap food in Victorian London. Here, the stallholder is keeping some oysters fresh in a tub of salt water, while he arranges open ones across his stall to tempt passing trade. The customer is eating an oyster straight from the shell. You can see a pepper shaker on the stall, used to season the oysters.

"Won't you have another one, John?"
Henry Mayhew: The oyster woman

"As to my customers, sir, why, indeed, they're all sorts. It's not a very few times that gentlemen (I call them so because they're mostly so civil) will stop – just as it's getting darkish, perhaps, and look about them, and then come to me. Ah! some of 'em will look, may be, like poor parsons down upon their luck, and swallow their oysters as if they was taking poison in a hurry. They'll not touch the bread or butter once in twenty times, but they'll be free with the pepper and vinegar, or they'll say quick and short, 'A crust off that.'

I many a time think that two penn'orth is a poor gentleman's dinner. It's the same often with a poor lady, with a veil that once was black over a bonnet to match, and shivering through her shawl. She'll have the same. About two penn'orth is the mark still; it's mostly two penn'orth. My son says it's because that's the price of a glass of gin, and some persons buy oysters instead – but that's only his joke, sir. It's not the vulgar poor that's our chief customers. There's many of them won't touch oysters, and I've heard some of them say that the sight of oysters makes them sick; like eating snails.

My heartiest customers, that I serve with the most pleasure, are working people, on a Saturday night. One couple I think the wife always goes to meet her husband on a Saturday night – has two, or three, or four penn'orth, and it's pleasant to hear them say, 'Won't you have another, John?' or, 'Do have one or two more, Mary Anne.' I've served them that way two or three years.

I send out a good many oysters, opened, for people's suppers, and sometimes for supper parties – at least I suppose so, for there's five or six dozen often ordered. The maidservants come for them then, and I give them two or three for themselves, but the very poor never buy of me – a penny buys a loaf, you see, or a ha'porth of bread and a ha'porth of cheese, or a half-pint of beer, with a farthing out. My customers are mostly working people and tradespeople. Some, mostly working people, take quantities of pepper with their oysters in cold weather, and say it's to warm them, and no doubt it does; but frosty weather is very bad oyster weather. The oysters gape and die, and then they are not so much as manure. **99**

Henry Mayhew: The customers of whelk sellers

66The chief customers for whelks are working people and poor people, and they prefer them to oysters: I do myself, and I think they're not so much eaten because they're not fashionable like oysters are. But I've sold them to first-rate public houses and to doctors' shops – more than to other shops, I don't know why – and to private houses. Masters have sent out their servant-maids to me for three or four pennies-worth for supper. I've offered the maids a whelk for themselves but they won't eat them in the street; I daresay they're afraid their young men may be about and might think they wasn't ladies if they eat whelks in the street. Boys are the best customers for small whelks, but if you don't look sharp they'll do you out of three halfpennies' worth of vinegar to a halfpenny of whelks. I can't make out why they like it so! They're particular enough in their way. If the whelks are thin, as they will be sometimes, the lads will say 'What a lot of snails you've gathered tonight!' If they're plump and fine, then they'll say 'Fat ones tonight – stunners!' The dust's a great injury to the trade in the summer time; it dries the whelks up and they look old.

The whelk shells are no use. Boys have asked me for them 'to make sea-shells of' they say – to hold them to their ears when they're big and there's a sound like the sea rolling. Gentlemen have sometimes told me to keep a dozen or twenty dozen, for borders to a garden. But I make no charge for them – just what a gentleman may please to give. 🙶

"Stale bread goes so very much further"
Henry Mayhew: A stale-bread seller

All the street sellers of bread started as bakers with baskets or barrows and their clothes always ingrained with fine dust from bread flour. They purchase stale bread from bakers' shops and sell it on to the poor, who can't afford fresh bread.

🙶It's a slave's life being a baker, so much night work, and the heat of the oven, with the close air and sleeping on sacks at nights, for you can't leave the place. A journeyman baker hasn't got what can be called a home for he's so much away at the oven, he'd better not be a married man for if his wife isn't very careful there's talk, and there's unhappiness about nothing, perhaps. A journeyman baker's life drives him to drink, almost whether he will or not – a street life's not quite so bad.

My customers are all poor persons – some in rags and some as decent as their bad earnings will let them. No doubt about it, there's poor women that buy of me, that's forced to live on stale bread. Where there's a family of children, stale bread goes so very much further. I think I sell to few but what has families, and I often hear my customers talk about their children and say they must make haste as the poor things are hungry, and they couldn't get them any bread sooner. I've had women come to me of an evening as soon as it was dusk and buy stale bread, as if they were ashamed to be seen. I sometimes have bread over and sell it for half of what it cost me, rather than hold it over to next day when it would be too stale. I have given it away to begging people and they would get something for it at a lodging house. Perhaps altogether I make about a guinea every week: wet weather and short days are against me. **99**

Henry Mayhew: An onion seller

Onions are twisted into ropes for street sale. The ropes are made of straw into which the onion roots are plaited and secured, this is done almost entirely by Irish women and girls. This is what one woman, about 35 years old, said.

"My two children, Biddy and Ned, ten and eight on their next birthdays, they help me with selling onions – I rope the onions for them. I buy the straw at a straw-dealer, twopence at a time makes six or twelve ropes according to the size. We do best with onions. Oranges is next, and nuts aren't nearly so good. The three of us now make a shilling and sometimes a shilling and sixpence a day, and that's grand doings. We may sell between us from two to three dozen ropes a day.**"**

"I don't do much in the nettle line"
Henry Mayhew: The chickweed seller

The old man was dressed in a ragged coat, with his hair and beard in wild disorder.

"I sell chickweed and groundsel, and turfs for caged larks: that's all I sell unless it's a few nettles that's ordered for someone's tea. I get the chickweed at Chalk Farm [a suburb of London], and I pay nothing for it, I get it out of the public fields. Every morning at about seven I go for it. The groundsel I get from a gentleman who gives me leave to take it from his garden; I get there every morning about nine. After I have my chickweed I generally gather enough of each to make up a dozen

THE GROUNDSEL MAN,

"Chick-weed and Grun-sell !"

The chickweed and groundsel seller who talked to Mayhew about his hard life is sketched here from a photograph taken at the time. Chickweed and groundsel are still fed to caged birds.

ha'penny bunches. The turf I buy: a young man calls here with them and I pay twopence a dozen for them. He cuts them himself and hires a barrow to take them about, selling the turfs to bird shops and to such as me.

I don't do much in the nettle line – there isn't much call for it. After I've gathered my things I put them in my basket and sling them at my back, and start around London. I cry 'chickweed and groundsel' as I go along – I don't say 'for young singing birds' although I know that's usual, but I never did. I've been at this business about eighteen years, and out every day until about five in the evening. I never stop to eat; I'm walking all the time. I have my breakfast before I start and my tea when I get home. But I can't go much above one mile and a half an hour owing to my right side being paralysed – my leg and foot and all is quite dead; I go along with a stick.

I sell to shops, but most to gentlefolk's houses, such people as keeps canaries or goldfinches or linnets. I charge a halfpenny a bunch for chickweed and groundsel together, that's the regular charge. The nettles are ordered in certain quantities and I don't get them unless they're ordered from ladies' houses. They consider the nettles to be good for their blood and they drink them in tea, mostly in the spring and autumn. The ladies I sell to are mostly sickly, but sometime they ain't, and have only a breakout on their skin or their faces.

Saturday is my best day, and I can't spare any time to gather on that day, I gather for Saturday on a Friday. On Saturday I daresay I get rid of two dozen bunches of chickweed and groundsel. On the other days sometimes I don't sell above five or six bunches.

In the summer I do better than in the winter – they give the food more often to their birds in summer, and change it oftener. **99**

"You can go in, Fishy!"
Henry Mayhew: A fried-fish seller

66I've been in the trade seventeen years. Before that I was a gentleman's servant and I married a servant maid, and we had a family, and on that account we couldn't either of us get a situation though we'd good characters. I was out of employ for seven or eight months and our things were going to the pawnshop for a living, but at last I gave up hope of getting into a gentleman's service, raised ten shillings, and determined to try something else. I was persuaded by a friend who kept a beer shop to sell oysters at his door, and I went to Billingsgate for the first time in my life and bought a peck of oysters for two shillings and sixpence.

I'd never been used to open oysters and I couldn't do it. I cut my fingers with the knife slipping all over them and had to hire a man to open for me, or the blood from my cut fingers would have run on the oysters. For all that I did well until in two or three months the oyster season was over and the same friend advised me to try fried fish. That suited me. I've lived in good families where there were first-rate men cooks and I know what good cooking means. I bought a dozen plaice and I started, and I stuck to it, and took from seven to ten shillings every night with more of course on Saturday, and it was half of it profit

This fish stall in a London street was photographed in 1877. The tall-crowned hat on the stallholder was very common in Victorian times: it is a kind of bowler, called a high round-top derby. You can see more bowler hats in the picture, and a top hat on the right.

then – I cleared a good mechanic's earnings at that time, thirty shillings a week and more.

I served the public houses and soon got known. With some landlords I could go into the parlour and taproom and bar when other tradesmen have been kept out. The landlords will say to me still: '*You* can go in, Fishy.' But the insults and difficulties I've had in the public-house trade are dreadful. One time I went into a bar and there was a party in the house, and one of the gents came down and gave my basket a kick without ever a word and started the fish out, and in a scuffle – he was a little fellow but my master – I had this finger put out of joint; you can see that still – and was in the hospital a week from the injury to my leg. I've had my tray kicked over for a lark in a public house, and a scramble for my fish and all gone, and no help and no money for me. The landlords always prevent such things when they can, and interfere for a poor man, but then it's done sudden and over in an instant.**"**

"No time to be clean"
Henry Mayhew: The smell of herrings

The rooms of the very poorest in London's population always smell of fish; most frequently of herrings. So much so, that to those who, like myself, have often visited their dwellings, the smell of herrings, even in comfortable homes, savours of squalor and wretchedness. The volatile oil of the fish seems to hang about the walls and beams of the rooms forever. Those who have experienced the smell of fish only in a clean bright kitchen, can have no idea of the stench, in a dilapidated and ill-drained house, and in a rarely cleaned room. I have many a time heard both husband and wife say that they had no time to be clean.

Costermongers supply the poor with every kind of fish, for they deal in every kind when it is cheap. Some deal only in such things as shrimps or periwinkles, but selling just one particular article is the exception and not the rule – and in any case, shrimps, lobsters and so on are rarely bought by the very poor.

The fish sent for sale in London is known as 'red fish' and 'white fish'. The red fish, as far as the metropolitan market is concerned, is confined to salmon, and all the other descriptions are known as white. The costermongers classify the fish they sell as wet and dry. All fresh fish is wet; while all cured or salted fish is dry.

The principal fish staple of the street-fishmonger is sole, which are in supply all (or nearly all) the year. The next staples are herrings, mackerel, whiting, Dutch eels, and plaice. The trade in plaice and sprats is almost entirely in the hands of the costermongers. Their sale of shrimps is nearer a half than a third of the entire quantity sent to Billingsgate Fish Market, but their purchase of cod, or of the best lobsters, or crabs, is far below a third. Costermongers rarely buy turbot, or brill, or even salmon, unless he can retail it at sixpence a pound. When it is at that price, a street salmon seller told me that the eagerness to buy it was extreme. He had known persons, who appeared to him to be very poor, buy a pound of salmon, just for a treat once in a way. His best, or rather readiest customers, were the shopkeepers of the busier parts, and the occupants of the smaller private houses of the suburbs. During the past year salmon was scarce and dear, and the costermongers bought, comparatively, none of it.

The stallholder on the left of this 1877 photograph is selling stone bottles of ginger beer. The man on the right with umbrellas under his arm is a mushfaker – a handyman who did odd jobs such as mending umbrellas. The word 'mushfaker' is said to come from 'mush', a slang term for an umbrella's mushroom shape, and 'faker', slang for someone who makes something seem fit to sell, even if it isn't. So a mushfaker might repair an umbrella to make it look as though it would work, even if it collapsed in the next shower of rain.

Henry Mayhew: The pie-men's cries

The pastries sold in the London streets are meat and fruit pies, boiled meat and kidney puddings, plum pudding, and an almost infinite variety of tarts, cakes, buns and biscuits. The pie-men go along with their pie cans in their arms, crying, 'Pies all hot! Penny pies, all hot!' The wandering street musicians often make their dinner off a meat pudding purchased on their rounds, for it is the rule with such people never to return home after starting in the morning, till their day's work is done.

'One a penny, two a penny, hot cross buns!
If your daughters will not eat them, give them to your sons.
But if you haven't any of those pretty little elves,
You cannot do better than eat them all yourselves.'

'One a penny poker, two a penny tongs!
One a penny, two a penny, hot cross buns.'

'One a penny, two a penny, hot Chelsea Buns!
Burning hot! Smoking hot! Reeking hot!
Hot Chelsea Buns!'

Henry Mayhew: The street sale of milk

During the summer months milk was sold in London markets, and on Sundays in Battersea Fields, Clapham Common, Camberwell Green, Hampstead Heath and similar places.

Ice cream was a new and exciting treat in 1877, because most people had never tasted frozen food. Those who knew what to expect laughed when novices bit into ice cream as they would into any other food. They got a shock when the cold confection hit their teeth and melted in their mouths.

About twenty men are engaged in this sale. They usually wear a smock frock and have the cans and yokes used by the regular milk sellers. The skim milk – for they sell none else – is purchased at the dairies at one and a halfpence a quart, and even the skim milk is further watered by the street sellers. Their cry is 'Half penny half pint! Milk!' The tin measure, however, in which the milk-and-water is served

*generally contains only half the quantity proclaimed. The
purchasers are chiefly boys and children, rarely men and
never costermongers 'for they reckon milk sickly'.*

*A pair of cans with the yoke costs fifteen shillings, and
one pound is amply sufficient as capital to start in this
trade, as the two measures used may be bought for two
shillings, and three shillings can be devoted to the
purchase of the liquid.*

*Curds and whey are a form of light refreshment
commonly associated with dairies. There is generally the
model of a cow in the front window, and sometimes
another on the counter. Where curds and whey are sold
there is also frequently a trade done in glasses of new milk
and milk and soda.*

CURDS AND WHEY When fresh milk is made into
cheese, a chemical called an enzyme is added to it.
The enzyme makes the milk separate into a watery
liquid called whey, and a thick grainy solid called
curds. It is the curd that is used to make cheese,
but in past times people also ate the curds and
whey – it was bit like yoghurt.

"It's dull sitting alongside a cow"
Henry Mayhew: The milk seller in St James's Park

*The sellers of milk in the Park draw the milk straight from
the cows' udders, as each customer requests. There are*

eight stands in the summer, and as many cows, but in the winter only four cows. The milk vendors sell on average from eighteen to twenty quarts a day in the summer, but in the winter not more than a third of that. The chief customers are infants, and adults and others of a delicate constitution who have been recommended to take new milk fresh from the cow. This milk seller was a sour-tempered woman.

66It's not at all a lively sort of life, selling milk from the cows, although some thinks so. I've often been dull enough, and could see nothing to interest me sitting alongside a cow. People drink new milk for their health, and I've served a good many such. They're mostly young women, I think, that's delicate, and makes the most of it. If they were set to some good hard work it would do them more good than new milk, or ass's milk either, I think. Let them go on a milk walk to cure them – that's what I say.

Some children come pretty regularly with their nurses to drink new milk. Some bring their own china mugs to drink it out of; nothing less was good enough for them. I've seen the nurse-girls frightened to death about the mugs. I've heard one young child say to another, 'I shall tell Mama that Caroline spoke to a mechanic, who came and shook hands with her.' The girl was as red as fire, and said it was her brother. Oh yes! There's a deal of 'brothers' come to look for their sisters in the Park! The greatest fools I've sold milk to are servant girls out for the day. Some must have a day or a half a day in a month – their mistresses ought to keep them at home, I say, and not let them out to spend their money and get into nobody knows what company for a holiday: mistresses are too easy that way. It's such girls that make fools of themselves in liking a soldier to run after them. I've seen one of them – some would call her pretty, and the prettiest is the silliest and easiest tricked out of her money, that's my opinion – I've seen one of them walk with a soldier and stop a minute, and she's taken something out of her glove and given it to him. Then they've come up to me and he's said to her, 'Mayn't I treat you with a little new milk my dear?' and he's changed a shilling. Why of course the silly fool of a girl had given him that there shilling! **99**

"A dictionary definition of milk"
Charles Dickens Jnr (the writer's son): A Dictionary of London, 1879

London milk sellers are supplied partly from cowsheds in London itself and partly from numerous farms in all parts of the country brought within easy reach by the railway system. Milk is, unfortunately, often the source or the means of spreading serious epidemics of typhoid, diphtheria, and scarlatina [a form of scarlet fever, a very dangerous infectious disease].

Henry Mayhew: Water carriers

It may surprise many to learn that there are still existing water carriers in London. Some of them depend on the trade for their livelihood, while others carry pails of spring water to the publicans or eating-house keepers, who may not have servants to send to the nearest pump for it and require it fresh and cool for those who drink it at their meals.

Henry Mayhew: Cold drinks

In hot weather there are two drink vendors who drive a big trade during the dinner-hour. These are the man with 'the yellow lemonade' in a big glass bottle (with the real lemon doing duty as a cork), and the sherbet vendor. An entirely new form of liquid refreshment for small boys has come into vogue during recent years. It is the liquor left in the preserved pineapple tin after the slices of fruit have been taken out. A halfpenny for a small glass is the price usually charged. The man who sells sarsaparilla as a beverage (which was also called 'saloop') uses a highly decorated stall on wheels, and wherever it stands it draws around it an admiring crowd.

SARSAPARILLA was a herbal drink made from an aromatic root, and was thought to be a great thirst-quencher in summer. It was very popular in Victorian times, especially as an alternative to alcoholic drinks.

A street scene in Cheapside, in East London, in 1900. The man in the foreground has an urn of hot water, and is offering sherbet and water drinks to passers-by. It's hard to see what the woman behind him has for sale in the large basket – it might be apples.

Henry Mayhew: The street sale of used tea leaves

One branch of the tea trade is closely connected with street life: that of tea leaves. The used leaves from the teapot are purchased from servants or poor women, and made into 'new' tea. The old tea leaves, to be converted into new ones, are dried out on hot plates, and then they are re-dyed. To give a green colour for green teas, a preparation of copper is used. For the black tea, no dye is usually necessary.

This re-manufactured tea is then sold to cheap shopkeepers, both in town and country, and is almost always sold ready mixed. The trade in old tea leaves is, I am assured, carried on quietly and cleverly and the most vigilant customs and excise officers are completely in the dark. One smaller 'tea-maker' was, however, fined for tea-leaf conversion last year.

GETTING AROUND LONDON

There were many forms of transport for Londoners in Mayhew's time, depending on how quickly people wanted to get anywhere, and how much money they had to spend. The railways moved people and goods faster than anything else – but that was just for getting in and out of London. Within the city, and in this time before motorcars, there were only two mechanized choices to make – the underground railway and the river steamers. Both of these involved steam engines. The Metropolitan & District Railway served London, and mostly ran in underground tunnels that encircled the city. This was the beginning of today's network of underground trains.

The little steamers that chugged up and down the river Thames were a popular feature of London life. One American visitor to London wrote this about them in 1852. 'Thousands, and tens of thousands, travel up and down the river by these little boats, because they are cheaper than the omnibuses, and in going by them, one avoids the noise of the streets. You can go from London Bridge, in the city, up to Westminster, near the Houses of Parliament, for a half penny, penny, or two pence, according to the line of boats you take. These boats are very small, and have no comfortable cabins for passengers, and all sit upon deck, no matter what the weather may be. This would not suit the American public, but Englishmen are, though great grumblers, not so luxurious in their tastes as we are – at least in such matters.'

In the outlying districts there were tramways – the trams were pulled by a team of horses. If you could afford one, you might choose to travel by horse-drawn cab. You could find cabs waiting at a cab rank or hail a cab in the street, just as you would today for a modern cab. Four-wheeled horse-drawn cabs were rather slow and uncomfortable, but they could hold four passengers – or five if one person sat outside with the driver. Two-wheeled cabs were called hansom cabs, and the driver sat outside at the back, driving his horses by holding the reins and whip over the top of the cab.

But the most popular transport option in London was the horse-drawn bus – called, in those days, an 'omnibus'. These began in London in 1829, and quickly became very popular. You could catch an omnibus just about anywhere in central London. The destinations were painted on the outside of the bus, and each omnibus was painted a different colour, depending on where it was going and who owned the bus company.

A guidebook to London, 1850

THE TOTAL NUMBER OF OMNIBUSES traversing the streets of LONDON is about 3,000, paying duty, including mileage, averaging nine pounds a month each. The number of conductors and drivers is about 7,000, paying annually £1,750 for their licences. The earnings of each vehicle vary from two pounds to four pounds a day. Be careful to observe the fares marked upon the outside; if you are in the least doubt, be sure and ask the conductor before you enter, otherwise you may be made to pay sixpence.

"There is nothing like an omnibus"
Charles Dickens: Sketches by 'Boz', 1836

The passengers change as often in the course of one journey as the figures in a kaleidoscope, and though not so glittering, are far more amusing. We believe there is no instance on record of a man's having gone to sleep in one of these vehicles. *Of all known vehicles, from the glass coach in which we were taken to be christened, to that sombre caravan in which we must one day make our last earthly journey, there is nothing like an omnibus. We will back the machine in which we make our daily peregrination from the top of Oxford Street to the city, against any 'bus' on the road, whether it be for the gaudiness of its exterior, the perfect simplicity of its interior, or the native coolness of its cad. [A 'cad' was the conductor who stood at the door of an omnibus to receive fares.] The cad's great boast is that he can 'chuck an old gentleman into the bus, shut him in, and rattle off, afore he knows where it's a-going to' – a feat which he frequently performs, to the infinite amusement of every one but the old gentleman concerned, who, somehow or other, never can see the joke of the thing.*

We are not aware that it has ever been precisely ascertained, how many passengers our omnibus will contain. The impression on the cad's mind evidently is, that it is amply sufficient for the accommodation of any number of persons that can be enticed into it. 'Any room?' cries a hot pedestrian. 'Plenty of room, sir,' replies the conductor, gradually opening the door, and not disclosing the real state of the case, until the wretched man is on the steps. 'Where?' inquires the entrapped individual, with an attempt to back out again. 'Either side, sir,' replies the cad, shoving him in, and slamming the door. 'All right, Bill!' Retreat is impossible; the newcomer rolls about till he falls down somewhere, and there he stops.

As we get into the city a little before ten, four or five of our party are regular passengers. We always take them up

The omnibus driver on the left is holding the long whip he uses to control his team of horses, while the man on the right with a short whip in his hand is the 'bus conductor. Perhaps he used his whip to discourage street boys and difficult passengers!

at the same places, and they generally occupy the same seats; they are always dressed in the same manner, and invariably discuss the same topics – the increasing rapidity of cabs, and the disregard of moral obligations evinced by omnibus men. There is a little testy old man, with a powdered head, who always sits on the right-hand side of the door as you enter, with his hands folded on the top of his umbrella. He is extremely impatient, and sits there for the purpose of keeping a sharp eye on the cad, with whom he generally holds a running dialogue. He is very officious in helping people in and out, and always volunteers to give the cad a poke with his umbrella, when anyone wants to alight. He usually recommends ladies to have sixpence ready, to prevent delay; and if anybody puts a window down that he can reach, he immediately puts it up again.

'Now, what are you stopping for?' says the little man every morning, the moment there is the slightest indication of 'pulling up' at the corner of Regent Street, when some such dialogue as the following takes place between him and the cad.

'What are you stopping for?'

(Here the cad whistles, and affects not to hear the question.)

'I say!' (a poke with the umbrella). 'What are you stopping for?'

'For passengers, sir.'

'Now mind,' exclaims the little old man, with great vehemence, 'I'll pull you up tomorrow; I've often threatened to do it; now I will.'

'Thankee, sir,' replies the cad, touching his hat with a mock expression of gratitude. 'Very much obliged to you indeed, sir.'

Here the young men in the omnibus laugh very heartily, and the old gentleman gets very red in the face. The stout gentleman in the white neckcloth, at the other end of the vehicle, looks very prophetic, and says that something must shortly be done with these fellows, or there's no saying where all this will end; and the shabby-genteel man with the green bag, expresses his entire concurrence in the opinion, as he has done regularly every morning for the last six months.

A second omnibus now comes up, and stops immediately behind us. Another old gentleman elevates his cane in the air, and runs with all his might towards our omnibus; we watch his progress with great interest; the door is opened to receive him, but he suddenly disappears – he has been spirited away by the opposition. The driver of the opposition taunts our people with his having 'regularly done 'em out of that old swell', and the voice of the 'old swell' is heard, vainly protesting against this unlawful detention.

We rattle off, the other omnibus rattles after us, and every time we stop to take up a passenger, they stop to take him too. Sometimes we get him; sometimes they get him; but whoever don't get him, say they ought to have had him, and the cads of the respective vehicles abuse one another accordingly. We drop a great many of our original passengers, and take up fresh ones, who meet with a very sulky reception. It is rather remarkable, that the people already in an omnibus always look at newcomers as if they have no business to come in at all. We are quite persuaded the little old man has some notion of this kind, and that he considers their entry as a sort of negative impertinence.

Conversation is now entirely dropped; each person gazes vacantly through the window in front of him, and everybody thinks that his opposite neighbour is staring at him. If one man gets out at Shoe Lane, and another at the *corner of Farringdon Street, the little old gentleman grumbles, and suggests to the latter, that if he had got out at Shoe Lane too, he would have saved them the delay of another stoppage. Whereupon the young men laugh again, and the old gentleman looks very solemn, and says nothing more till he gets to the Bank, when he trots off as fast as he can, leaving us to do the same, and to wish, as we walk away, that we could impart to others any portion of the amusement we have gained for ourselves.*

A guidebook to London, 1844

OMNIBUSES ARE OF FOREIGN ORIGIN. Travelling the town upon all the leading lines of the metropolis, are a great public convenience. They are, nevertheless, a great nuisance in the streets through which they run, from the noise occasioned by their perpetual passage. The charges vary from sixpence to one shilling, but strangers in London should, upon all occasions, previous to entering them, make enquiry, a caution that will prove productive of relief from much trouble and annoyance.

The photograph was taken in 1887, when decorations to mark Queen Victoria's Golden Jubilee were being put up in Ludgate Circus in east London. (You can see the ladders propped against the main building.) There are three different forms of transport passing this busy place, including an open-topped omnibus.

Punch *magazine, 1849: Children must be paid for!*

In 1849 the omnibus companies decided that children – who had been carried free until that time – must be paid for in future. This caused a storm of argument and controversy amongst the customers of omnibus companies. This letter to *Punch* magazine in 1849 makes fun of the whole thing.

SIR,

'CHILDREN MUST BE PAID FOR'

Such is the sensible law now of certain Omnibuses! Mothers tremble as they read it. Grandmothers pout and shake with suppressed rage as they point out the offensive document to their offended daughters. In the meantime the new code has effected a great revolution in our public vehicles. The north and west Ridings of London are much quieter, and a gentleman can really dismount now from his horse, and enter a Two-penny Omnibus in peace without fear of being hemmed in with a baby on each side of him, besides having a little prodigy deposited in his lap, in addition to the comfort of having a couple of twins opposite staring him out of countenance. The latter infliction I have always

---

looked upon as one of the most fearful sights of the metropolis, for I have particularly noticed that when a baby takes a fancy to stare at you, it will do so for hours, and that nothing will induce it to take its little eyes off your face but a penny bun, or a bunch of keys to swallow, or some act of great violence.

Since the march of reform has turned its steps in the direction of the Omnibuses, I should like a few more improving placards to be suspended inside.

The following one is indispensable: 'NO POODLES ADMITTED'. It is not agreeable to have an ugly beast of a French dog looking at one in this warm weather. I beg to say I hate poodles at any time, and dislike them still more in a shut-up carriage, when they will keep eyeing your calf in a most wistful manner, as much as to say, 'Shouldn't I like to have a bit!' It makes me nervous.

I should like to see 'ALL BUNDLES, BASKETS, AND CAGES, RIGIDLY EXCLUDED'. Washerwomen have got into the shameful habit of carrying their Saturday's linen inside the Omnibus; and I have seen the melancholy instance of a fine young fellow turning quite pale upon beholding a false front drop out of the basket with his name written in full in the corner of it. Then bundles are always in the way, and the ladies who bring them in always think that they should be the last persons who ought to have the trouble of carrying them.

I have only one more suggestion to make. 'GENTLEMEN ARE REQUESTED TO KEEP THEIR WET UMBRELLAS BETWEEN THEIR OWN LEGS'. This is a nuisance that must be felt to be appreciated. In my many journeys through life I have experienced that man is too apt to thrust his drenched umbrella between the legs of his neighbours. The practice is, I am aware, a very old one, but cannot be defended upon any footing whatever.

Omnibuses may then, when they are properly ventilated, and carry precisely half their present number, and are severely fined every time they stop, be made endurable; but the tax upon babies is certainly a great blessing. The sooner all the other nuisances are thrown after the children, the better.

I remain, Sir, (And hope all my life to remain so),

A CONFIRMED BACHELOR.

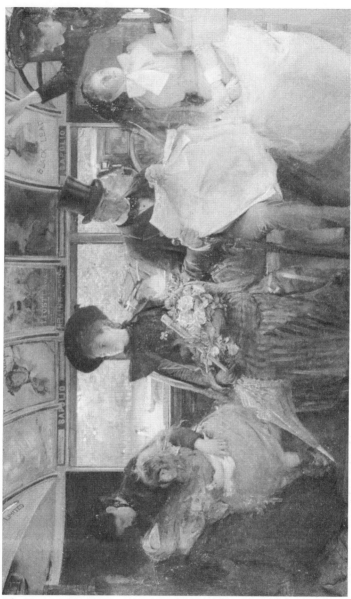

'The Bayswater Omnibus' was painted in 1895 by George William Joy, and shows a group of passengers inside a horse-drawn omnibus. Everyone looks very prosperous and respectable. Advertising posters line the roof of the 'bus.

"No rest for the driver"
Henry Mayhew: The omnibus driver

Drivers must produce testimonials as to their possessing the necessary skill. They are not to gallop their horses under any circumstances whatsoever. They are required, moreover, to drive slowly in the markets and narrow streets. They must as much as possible, keep the wheels of their vehicle out of the gutters.

❝It's hard work is mine, for I never have any rest but a few minutes, except every other Sunday and then only two hours; that's the time of a journey there and back. If I was to ask leave to go to church and then go to work again I know what the answer would be – 'You can go to church as often as you like, and we can get a man who doesn't want to go there.' I must keep exact time at every place where a time-keeper's stationed. Not a minute's excused – there's a fine for the least delay. I can't say that it's often levied, but still we are liable to it. If I've been blocked, I must make up that block by galloping, and if I'm seen to gallop, and anybody tells our people I'm called over the coals. I must drive as quick with a thunder-rain pelting in my face and the roads in a muddle, and the horses starting at every flash, just as quick as if it was a fine hard road and fine weather. It's not easy to drive a bus, but I can drive, and must drive to an inch – yes, to half an inch. I know if I can get my horses' heads through a space I can get my splinter-bar through. I drive by my pole, making it my centre. If I keep it fair in the centre a carriage must follow – unless it's slippery weather and then there's no calculating.

It's very hard work for the horses. The starting after stopping is the hardest work for them, it's such a terrible strain. I've felt for the poor things on a wet night with a bus full of big people. A bus changes horses four or five times a day, according to the distance. There's no cruelty to the horses, not a bit, it wouldn't be allowed. Every horse in our stables has one day's rest in every four, but it's no rest for the driver. **99**

From Lewis Carroll's scrapbook

TO CABMEN.—An UMBRELLA, left in a cab which was taken to Lower Eaton Street from the Strand, on Sunday night, 27th inst., between 11 and 12 o'clock p.m., is anxiously EXPECTED at 6, Northumberland Street, Strand, where a REWARD and the blessings of the owner await the honest restorer.

Albert Smith: The art of the crossing sweeper

A little time ago, one Sunday, we saw a man at the entrance to Hyde Park, who had swept the dirt into all sorts of figures – hearts, diamonds, circles, and stars, until the road was an exhibition in itself.

But before this, one winter, a very elaborate crossing was made by a man in the new street that runs from St Giles' into Long Acre. He had established his right of way in front of a hoarding opposite the church that has been erected there; and had hedged it with sprigs of holly stuck into the ground. At night it was perfectly brilliant, with inches of candle and small tallow lamps placed along it. You were compelled to find a halfpenny, however cold and irksome the operation of unbuttoning your coat to hunt after it might be.

Before long he found as many imitators as a man always does who strikes out a new line in anything; and the whole street was a succession of swept pathways. It would have required more coppers than an able-bodied individual could have conveniently carried, to have satisfied the claimants.

CROSSING SWEEPERS provided a sort of public service in the streets of Victorian cities. In return for small tips from the people who used their services, road and crossing sweepers brushed the dirt and rubbish out of the way before they stepped into the road.

Charles Manby Smith: The professional crossing sweeper

The top rank of street sweepers are bred to the business, and have followed it from earliest infancy. Such a man

A cartoon from *Punch* magazine in the 1860s:
Rich woman: 'No, I've nothing for you. You always ask me every time I cross.'
Crossing boy: 'Yes, and every time you crosses you allus gives me nothink!'

*has never dreamed of pursuing any other calling He
claims precedence before all others, as being to the
manner born, and inherits his broom from his father, or
mother, as it might be. All his ideas, interests, and
affections are centred in one spot of ground – the spot he
sweeps, and has swept daily for the last twenty or thirty*

years, ever since it was bequeathed to him by his parent. He knows every inmate of every house in his immediate neighbourhood; and not only that, but he knows their private history and antecedents for the last twenty years. He has watched a whole generation growing up under his broom, and he looks upon them all as so much material destined to enhance the value of his estate. He is the humble pensioner of a dozen families: he wears the shoes of one, the stockings of another, the shirts of a third, the coats of a fourth, and so on. He recognizes everybody's cat and everybody's dog, and will carry them home if he finds them straying. He does everybody's serving maids a thousand kind offices (repaid with interest by surreptitious scraps from the larder, and hot tea in the cold wintry afternoons). He is part and parcel of the street view, and where he goes when he leaves his station, you have not the least notion. He is there so soon as it is light in the morning, and till long after the gas is burning at night.

Female crossing sweepers are almost entirely divided between children or young girls, and women above the age of forty. The children rarely stay for many weeks together in a single spot, and so lose the advantage of the charitable interest they would produce in persons who were used to meeting them regularly in their walks. But for the most part, these are children of parents in extremely low circumstances, who send them forth with a broom to pick up a few halfpence to assist them in the daily provision for the family.

The older women, on the other hand, of whom there are many scattered throughout London, think it very important to stay constantly in one spot, and would dread to lose a connection they have been many years in forming. Many will even cling to it after it has ceased to be a thoroughfare by the opening of a new route, unless they can discover the new routes their patrons have taken.

The exceptions to these two groups – the old and the very young – will be found to consist mostly of young widows left with the charge of an infant family. The spectacle of a young mother, with an infant on one arm muffled up from the driving rain, while she plies a broom single-handed, is one which appeals to the sympathies of a London public. It is these poor widows who, by rearing their orphaned offspring to wield the broom, supplement the ranks of the professional sweepers. In 1841, one of these women was left a widow with three small children, the eldest under four, and the youngest in arms. Clad in deep mourning, she took up a position at an angular crossing of a square, and was allowed to accommodate the two elder children upon some matting spread upon the steps of a door. With the infant in one arm, she plied her broom with the other, and held out a small white hand for the reception of such charity as the passers-by might choose to bestow. The children grew up strong and hearty, in spite of their exposure to the weather at all seasons. All three of them are at the present moment sweepers in the same line of route, at no great distance from the mother, who, during the whole period, has scarcely abandoned her post for a single day. We have frequently met the four returning home together in the deepening twilight, the elder boy carrying the four brooms strapped together on his shoulder.

"The good times is all gone"
Henry Mayhew: A woman crossing sweeper

66Fifteen years I've been on the crossing, come next Christmas. The poor woman who had it before me was killed, so I took it. The first day I took sixpence, but them good times is all gone, they'll never come back again. The best times I used to take a shilling a day, and now I don't take but a few pence. People going to their offices at six and seven in the morning give me a ha'penny or a penny; if they don't I must go without it. I go at five, and stand there till eleven or twelve, till I find it is no use being there any longer. Gentlemen give me the most, I'm sure; the ladies don't give me nothing. I stand on my crossing 'til I'm like to drop over my broom with tiredness. I never get spoken to on my road; only some people say 'Good morning', or 'There you are old lady'. They never asks me no questions. I never get run over, though I am very hard of hearing, but I am forced to have my eyes here, there and everywhere, to keep out of the way of the carts and coaches.

I get two shilling a week from the parish, and I have to pay out of that for bread, sugar and tea. A shilling goes for my lodging, they let me come there instead of wandering about the streets. I'm eighty years of age and I couldn't do hard work. To do a hard day's washing – I couldn't. I used to go to a lady's house to do a bit of washing when I had my strength, but I can't do it now. If I was to go into the Poor House I shouldn't live three days. It's not that I eat much – a very little is enough for me. But it's the air I should miss. To be shut up like a thief, I couldn't live long, I know. 99

196

AFTERWORD

It is easy for us to criticize the past and say what's wrong with a society that isn't our own – and there is a lot to criticize about Victorian London. The conditions in which many people lived and worked were shocking: we wouldn't tolerate them now. Those who had jobs were often not much better off than slaves; some young children worked sixteen hours or more a day. But it was even worse to have no job at all and still try to support yourself and your family.

The basic human rights we think are important – such as free healthcare and education, decent housing, and equal opportunities for everyone – were unknown to the people in this anthology. Modern inventions like space travel and the Internet would probably make them gasp in wonder and disbelief, but so would many everyday things we take for granted like domestic electricity and water supplies, and supermarkets. Yet the Victorian era was the beginning of the modern world: the beginning of our world, in fact, though you might not think so.

The social and industrial changes that swept through Britain during the reign of Queen Victoria transformed everyday life. Farmers and labourers flocked to cities like London in search of work, looking for relief from the bitter hardships of the countryside. They travelled by foot on dusty unpaved roads, and slept where they could find shelter. By the end of the nineteenth century the descendants of those farmers and villagers were travelling on a network of railways above and below the ground, and commuting from the outskirts of the cities. There were extraordinary increases in wealth and poverty, and in both success and suffering. The Industrial Revolution that flourished in Victorian Britain produced a new society, based in the towns and built on machinery and mass production. That society laid the foundations of our own times – and of centuries yet to come.

Mayhew's interviews help us to understand the problems of Victorian society, and they helped many Victorians to understand them, too. Social reformers used his evidence to press for change, and by the time the Victorian era ended in 1901 many of the worst conditions of the time had been changed or abolished.

INDEX OF ENTRIES

FURTHER INFORMATION

1. Henry Mayhew's books

Henry Mayhew's first article about the people who lived and worked on the streets of London appeared in a newspaper called the *Morning Chronicle* on 18 October 1849. More articles appeared in the newspaper every day for the rest of 1849, and for most of 1850 as well. Mayhew himself wrote at least two of these articles a week, although some of them were written by other journalists. In 1851, Henry Mayhew's collected articles on poverty were published as a book in four volumes, called *London Labour and the London Poor*. Copies of that first edition, or one of the many nineteenth-century reprints, are still kept in some reference libraries, although they are now too old and fragile to be borrowed. But new editions of Mayhew's work have recently been published, many with illustrations. Three of the best of these are:

London Labour and the London Poor: A Selection, edited by Victor E. Neuburg, Penguin, 1985
Henry Mayhew: London Characters and Crooks, selected and edited by Christopher Hibbert, Folio Society, 1997
The Illustrated Mayhew's London, edited by John Canning, Weidenfeld and Nicolson, 1986

2. Other sources used in this anthology
London and Londoners in the Eighteen-Fifties and Sixties, by Alfred Rosling Bennett, T. Fisher Unwin, 1924
Picked up in the Streets, or Struggles for Life amongst the London Poor, by Richard Rowe, WH Allen, 1880
Gavarni in London: Sketches of Life and Character, edited by Albert Richard Smith, Bogue, 1849

The Little World of London, or Pictures in Little of London Life, by Charles Manby Smith, Hall, 1857
The Seven Curses of London, by James Greenwood, Stanley Rivers, 1889
The Terrible Sights of London, by Thomas Archer, Stanley Rivers, 1870

3. Other books about Victorian London
Victorian London Street Life in Historic Photographs, by John Thomson & Adolphe Smith, Dover Publications, 1994
In Their Own Words: The Victorians, by Robert Hull, Franklin Watts, 2003

4. Novels for young readers set in Victorian London
Smith, by Leon Garfield, Puffin Modern Classics, 2004
The Ruby in the Smoke, *The Shadow in the North*, *The Tiger in the Well* and *The Tin Princess*, all by Philip Pullman, Scholastic Point, 2004

5. Internet resources
www.victorianlondon.org is an excellent web site called 'The Victorian Dictionary – the social history of Victorian London'. It's run by Lee Jackson, who also writes detective novels set in that time.
www.spartacus.schoolnet.co.uk/Jmayhew.htm is a good basic page about Henry Mayhew.
www.cityofshadows.stegenga.net is an interesting site with lots of atmospheric material.
www.victorianweb.org has a range of links to yet more historical sites.

INDEX

ACKNOWLEDGMENTS

Page 8 Private Collection/The Bridgeman Art Library; Page 14 Pictures of coins reproduced by courtesy of the Royal Mint; Page 18 Private Collection/The Bridgeman Art Library; Page 28 Victoria & Albert Museum, London, UK/The Bridgeman Art Library; Page 38 Private Collection/The Bridgeman Art Library; Pages 48, 63 and 67 Mary Evans Picture Library; Page 70 Victoria & Albert Museum, London, UK/The Bridgeman Art Library; Page 79 The Ann Ronan Picture Library/Heritage-Images; Pages 84, 87 and 93 Mary Evans Picture Library; Page 98 V&A Images/Victoria & Albert Museum; Pages 101 and 116 Mary Evans Picture Library; Page 130 The British Library; Pages 138, 141, 152, 156, 162 and 165 Mary Evans Picture Library; Page 168 Victoria & Albert Museum, London, UK/The Bridgeman Art Library; Page 170 Mary Evans Picture Library; Page 175 Private Collection/The Stapleton Collection/The Bridgeman Art Library; Page 181 Mary Evans Picture Library; Page 185 Private Collection/The Stapleton Collection/The Bridgeman Art Library; Page 189 Museum of London, UK/The Bridgeman Art Library.

Every effort has been made to trace copyright holders, but sometimes we have been unsuccessful. We would be grateful to hear from any copyright holder not acknowledged so that we can correct this omission at the first opportunity.

Belinda Hollyer has been a teacher, a school librarian and a children's publisher, and is now a full-time writer and anthologist. She has been fascinated by Henry Mayhew's books for many years, and seized the opportunity to create a brand-new anthology for young readers.

Praise for Belinda Hollyer
and *Haven't You Grown!*
'An inspired collection of
poems – this is a flawless
anthology for 5–11 year-olds.'
The Telegraph